Russell D. Longcore

# COMMERCIAL INSURANCE CLAIM SECRETS

## *REVEALED!*

**TAKE CONTROL OF YOUR BUSINESS INSURANCE CLAIMS! ADD HUNDREDS OR THOUSANDS MORE DOLLARS TO YOUR CLAIM SETTLEMENT!**

Order this book online at: www.insurance-claim-secrets.com or
www.amapublishing.com

AMA Publishing titles are available at major online book retailers.

Library of Congress Control Number:

ISBN: 978-0-615-32089-2

Manufactured in the United States of America

10   9 8 7 6 5 4 3 2 1

# AMA

ABIGAIL MORGAN AUSTIN PUBLISHING COMPANY
1750 POWDER SPRINGS ROAD, SUITE 190
MARIETTA, GEORGIA 30064
PHONE 678-234-2923  FAX 877-688-5879
WWW.AMAPUBLISHING.COM
E: AMAPUBLISHINGCO@GMAIL.COM

Book review by Reg Nordman, Managing Partner of Rocket Builders, a Canadian I.T. sales company. (www.regnordman.com)

*"Commercial Insurance Claim Secrets Revealed!"* by Russell D. Longcore. 2009.

"This is much more than just an overview of the commercial insurance market. This serves as an easy-to-grasp handbook for anyone who has to deal with commercial insurance. The author has been in the game for a long time and already wrote a book *("Insurance Claim Secrets REVEALED!")* on consumer insurance that is doing quite well. I was able to validate many of the costly lessons learned over many years in business and as a Condominium Strata Council member. The book is useful regardless of Canadian or US insurance rules. There are only a very few US-specific examples used. **If you are a growing company or a mature one and you have insurance, your HR/Ops Departments should have a copy of this book. It should save you money."**

\* \* \* \* \* \* \* \* \* \* \* \* \*

"Russell Longcore has again come to the rescue of the consumer with *"Commercial Insurance Claim Secrets Revealed!"* Russell tells the insider industry secrets that the insurance companies DO NOT WANT YOU TO KNOW! I met Russell many years ago when he was breaking into the insurance industry. He has gone on to have a passion for the consumer when it comes to insurance. I must say frankly, that NO ONE SHOULD BUY INSURANCE OF ANY KIND without first reading this book. Reading Russell's books has saved me thousands of dollars in not only personal insurance decisions, but in my business insurance also. Read this book and pass it along to your family. You'll be glad you did!"

Cary L. Wise
Owner
Rowafil USA, Biological Water Reclamation
Hondo, Texas

## Disclaimer

The information in this book is general in nature and does not take into account each and every situation that could possibly arise. You must thoroughly review your own insurance policy to determine your rights and responsibilities, and the rights and responsibilities of the insurance company. The information provided herein is intended to be current and accurate. However, such information may not be sufficient to deal with your individual situation.

Abigail Morgan Austin Publishing Company, the author, contributors or distributors do not warrant, guarantee or represent in any manner that the information presented herein is suitable for you. No portion of this book is intended to provide you with legal advice regarding your individual policy or claim. The information herein is meant to assist and guide you, and should not be relied upon as a substitute for independent research, tax and legal advice. Before acting on our advice, we recommend that you seek legal counsel from your attorney.

The laws governing each state will not only vary, but are continuously subject to change. We strongly urge you to seek legal advice before taking any action.

**Cover art beautifully done by Daniel Wright at:**

**www.createdwright.com**

This book is dedicated to my Redhead, Julia Ann.

You are the greatest love of my life.

## A note from the author

My first book, *"Insurance Claim Secrets REVEALED!"* was written primarily for consumers. It deals with consumer claims, such as homeowners, auto and liability.

But many of the strategies for handling claims are the same for commercial entities as they are for consumers.

Consequently, if you read both books, you will find that much of the content of the first book is re-purposed in this book and tailored for Commercial insurance strategies.

I hope you enjoy the book. But most of all, I hope that you use the book as a tool to assist you in recovering all of the money you are entitled to collect under the terms and conditions of your policy.

# Table of Contents

# INTRODUCTION

There's a little song that says, "Love makes the world go around." I hate to be the one to tell you this…but that's not true.

There's also a song in the musical "Cabaret", that says, "Money makes the world go around." That's a little closer to reality, but still not all the way true.

Insurance makes the world go around.

Nearly everything that we touch, and nearly everything that touches us, is insured. Without insurance, most of the everyday products and services we just accept as normal could only be purchased by the wealthy. Without insurance, businesses could not protect themselves from liability lawsuits. There would not be thousands of ships that carry cargo between nations, as investors in the ships and the cargo could not be sure they wouldn't be financially wiped out if their ships sank on the high seas.

If it weren't for insurance, very few people would ever get a home mortgage or an automobile loan. Think about it….what bank would lend YOU money for a house when their collateral might burn to the ground? Same for a car…what bank would lend money when the car could be destroyed in an accident?

Closer to home, people who were found to be negligent in a court of law would be financially wiped out making restitution to their victims. People would be reluctant to even drive their car to the market for fear of getting in an accident that was their fault.

Our world would be very different, and the world's capitalist system of economics would be radically different without insurance. Just think of how world economics worked just 400 years ago in the days before insurance was invented.

That's what our world would still be like today without insurance.

A significant portion of every business' income is spent for insurance. We insure our buildings, our contents, our inventory, our business income, our employees and their health, our lives, our vehicles and our liability to others.

Have you ever heard the term "insurance poor?" That's the feeling one gets when he sees a large portion of his disposable income paid out in insurance premiums. It usually also means that the person doesn't think that they're getting their money's worth. I say that because people don't usually complain about the price of something if they perceive that the value is worth the price. I've heard LOTS of business owners say that they're "insurance poor," and I know how they feel.

Yet, for all of the money that businesses spend on insurance, hardly anyone understands how it works. Fewer still ever read the policies that they buy. That lack of understanding leaves the business owners and managers very vulnerable, and likely to receive far less money in any insurance settlement than the amount that they are entitled to collect.

Before you go any further, let me tell you a little bit about me.

I've been around the insurance business since 1973. In late 1972, my wife and I bought our first house for $21,500.00. Three little bedrooms, one bath, 1008 square feet on a half-acre lot. It wasn't much, but it was ours. Naturally, we bought a homeowners insurance policy just before closing...the bank required it. In January of 1973, Gary Sherman, the Farm Bureau Insurance agent who sold the policy came to the house one evening to deliver the policy, and try to sell us auto and life insurance. I don't remember if he was successful that night in selling us more insurance, but he asked me if I'd be interested in becoming an insurance agent.

I was nineteen years old, working as a laborer in my father's construction company, in January in Michigan. I wasn't real excited about working outdoors, and didn't see much future in it. This guy was offering me inside work...wearing a coat and tie.

What do you <u>think</u> I said?

YES!!!

By the end of April, I had passed my state licensing exams, and gotten my agent licenses. I was on my way as a Farm Bureau Insurance agent.  I was the youngest agent that the company had ever hired in their history. Soon after that, Gary and his manager Jim Wood3 moved down the street and started an independent agency. I joined them.

After five years, I went back into the family construction business, and eventually became Vice President of the three construction companies we owned. I always kept my licenses active, and sold various types of insurance on a part-time basis.

In 1986, I sold my portion of the construction companies back to my Dad, and went back into insurance sales full-time. I sold term life insurance and investment securities, and did pretty well.

In 1992, we moved from West Michigan to Atlanta, Georgia. Shortly after arriving here in Atlanta, Hurricane Andrew devastated South Florida and Louisiana. The insurance companies were completely overloaded with claims, as were the independent claims adjusting companies that served those insurance companies. In those instances, insurance companies and adjusting companies rely heavily on temporary adjusters…"storm troopers," as they are called. The companies look for people with either insurance experience or construction experience.

I had both.

A national independent adjusting company hired me immediately, and in a few days I was in Miami.

What an amazing experience catastrophe adjusting (CAT duty) was!! I remember, on my first day, standing on the roof of a one story house in Kendall, Florida, measuring and making a diagram of what was left of the roof. I looked up, and as far as the eye could see in every direction were roofs with blue tarps on them.

Even right then, I knew I would love claims adjusting.

I could hardly believe that someone was going to pay me a lot of money to look at damages and write estimates. I'd been writing estimates for years. I thought I'd died and gone to heaven.

(I hope that you have work that you love. Most of the people that I know don't like what they do for a living.)

Once the CAT duty was over, I came back to Atlanta, and soon I'd found a full-time job with an independent adjusting company. I've been a claims adjuster ever since.

I've had some of the best training in claims that a fellow could possibly get. The companies I worked for kept sending me to various schools, each one more advanced than the last. I also did a lot of study through trade institutes. That helped me rocket forward in the claims business.

For a couple of years, I even did work for an insurance company as Home Office General Adjuster and property Claims Examiner. I got an insider's look at how claims are processed in an insurance company claims department. Boy, did my eyes get opened by that experience! It's one thing to investigate a claim as an adjuster, and then send a report to a claims examiner at the insurance company. It's a whole different experience to be the claims examiner, making the decisions on what is covered and what is not covered...what claims get paid, how much gets paid, and what claims get denied.

One of the most important things that I learned as a Claims Examiner was that people were usually not very impressed with the adjuster that handled their claim. The best adjusters are detail oriented, curious and self-motivated. Unfortunately, many adjusters are not thorough, seldom curious, and somewhat lazy. Most of the reports I received were mediocre in quality. There were a notable few adjusters who did a superb job.

I think I've adjusted just about every kind of claim you could think of...homeowners, automobile, worker's compensation, ocean cargo, trucking, inland marine, jeweler's block, liability, business income, commercial property...and loved every minute of it. The money hasn't been bad, either.

There's a position in the claims adjusting field that's called a "General Adjuster," or GA. It's kind of like being a General in the military. The GA position is as high as an adjuster can go. To qualify, you have to take a lot of insurance coursework, have a peer review of your claims handling work, and have a depth of experience.

It normally takes an adjuster at least ten to fifteen years to attain this position. I made it in four years. In 2005, I've became an Executive General Adjuster. That means I handled the most complicated and huge losses, and supervise the work of other adjusters.

In 2006, I wrote a pro-consumer book about insurance claims entitled *"Insurance Claim Secrets REVEALED!"* I was tired of seeing policyholders get short-changed by the insurance companies and decided to do something about it.

While the book was still in manuscript form, I showed it to the president of the company where was working at the time. I had even written the book under an assumed name, since everyone who had seen the manuscript told me that I couldn't stay working on the insurance company side if I published the book.

That company fired me just for writing the manuscript! So, I released the book in my own name in June 2007. It certainly hit a responsive chord in North America. By October 2007, the book had soared to Number One in two categories at Amazon.com. The book has remained Number One continuously since October 2007. And, of over 340,000 books available at Amazon related to insurance, my book is consistently in the top 100. The book has sold all over the world.

Now, in 2009, I've become a Claims Consultant. As a Claims Consultant I bill my hourly time at $175 - $200 per hour. I'll tell you more about that in Chapter One. I have clients all over the US and Canada.

Friends, I'm haven't told you all of this history to brag. I'd just like you to feel confident that I know what I'm talking about in the insurance sales and the insurance claims businesses.

Just like you, I've been an insurance consumer all of my adult life…even earlier, as a teenager with my first car, a '59 Jeep. But, unlike most of you, I've had the chance to experience both sides of the insurance world…. as a consumer and business owner, then as an agent and adjuster.

**Here's exactly why I wrote this new book and my first book,** *"Insurance Claim Secrets REVEALED!"* Most of the people for whom I've adjusted claims had never had a property or casualty insurance claim before. (We're not dealing with health or life insurance in this book.) Most of those same people had NEVER read their policy, even after filing the claim. They had no idea what the claims process was, and they relied on me...the adjuster...to walk them through the process.

It is for you, and people just like you that I write this book. Many times, people who have had a loss are on the raw edge of emotion. Isn't is natural to be fearful in a situation where you don't feel you're in control...where you don't know what will happen next, and you're scared you'll be "ripped off?" Most everyone has heard a story from a relative or friend about an insurance claim that went badly.

Business owners have even more complications. You have to keep the business afloat and viable. You rely on your sales for your business income. You have employees that count on their paychecks. You may be a business that is a supplier. What happens if you cannot fill your orders? Will your customers go to other vendors?

I've seen LOTS of businesses close their doors after a major loss, and it does not have to happen.

People like that need solid advice and a strategy on what to do to get their claim paid.

They need to understand the claims process completely so that they are not at the mercy of the insurance company, the claims adjuster and the claims examiner.

They need to be paid every dollar that they are entitled to collect.

They need to have peace of mind knowing that their claim was handled correctly.

Insurance companies rely upon the ignorance of their own policyholders. So do many claims adjusters. Insurance companies can increase their profits on your lack of knowledge. An uninformed policyholder will rarely argue with an adjuster, <u>because the policyholders don't know what they don't know.</u>

Let me repeat that phrase so you can think about it long and hard.

<u>MOST POLICYHOLDERS OR CLAIMANTS DON'T KNOW WHAT THEY DON'T KNOW.</u>

They don't know what is in their insurance policy, and they don't know the claims process, and that lack of knowledge can cost them thousands in settlement dollars and <u>all of their peace of mind.</u>

Everything that you must do to file a claim is in your insurance policy. WHAT'S MISSING IS HOW TO DO IT.

Think of it this way: I hand you a blueprint for a small house, and tell you, "Build this house over there on that lot." I've told you WHAT to do…I've even given you a document that tells you what must be done. WHAT'S MISSING IS HOW TO TAKE THAT BLUEPRINT AND BUILD THE HOUSE.

Do you know how to pour concrete or lay cement blocks?

Do you know how to install shingles?

Do you know how to install electrical wiring?

You may build a house, but it probably won't look anything like what's on that blueprint.

If you've never built a house before, you won't know what to do first…or next…or last.

House building takes experience. Or it takes very detailed instructions on how to build a house…step by step with no steps left out.

If you have NO EXPERIENCE in house building, then you must either rely on someone who does have that experience, or you must follow step-by-step instructions…or some combination of both.

<u>That principle is exactly the same in filing an insurance claim of any type</u>. It doesn't matter if you're in the United States, or Canada, or Brazil, or Panama, or Germany, or France, or Egypt, or South Africa, or China, or India.

It doesn't matter if your claim is a Commercial Property loss, or Liability, or Inland Marine, or Motor Truck Cargo, or whatever kind of claim you may have. If you have NO experience in filing a claim successfully, and getting every dollar you're entitled to collect, then you must rely on either someone who does have that experience, or <u>you must follow the step-by-step instructions IN THIS BOOK</u>…or some combination of both.

I believe that what you don't know <u>can hurt you</u>…it could even change the course of your life. I believe that your lack of knowledge about the claims process could change the destiny of your children's lives and generations into the future.

For example, consider a man who owns a small business. The building that houses the business burns to the ground, and every shred of his business records burn with it. The owner didn't know that they had to keep the business insured to value, and did not have enough coverage. So the insurance company hits them with a co-insurance penalty that reduces their settlement by a big percentage. (This topic is explored in Chapter Twenty Six.) The owner did not do a good job of taking inventory of his business personal property. Now they are forced to do it from memory, as the contents are now ashes. The building and contents are not insured for replacement cost, and the claim is settled for Actual Cash Value, or depreciated dollars.

The owner of the business cannot replace his inventory, machinery, equipment, office furnishings and building for the amount of money the insurance company paid him. He either has to borrow the money to get back in business, or close the doors.

And, that doesn't take into account any delays by the insurance company.

This business owner and his family have their lives permanently altered for the rest of their lives. The owner has to get a job working for someone else. Because of the fire, there's no money for college, and the children don't go to college.

And how about the lives of his employees?

Everybody in that story suffered because the owner was not prepared. Even the grandchildren yet unborn will have their lives affected because their parents did not get a college degree, and that affected their parents' ability to earn a higher income.

You see? One loss, not properly handled, can affect your destiny and your children's destiny, and generations to come. You may accuse me of melodrama, but you know that this stuff happens regularly.

**Read this book, and make sure it doesn't happen to you.**

Remember the scene in the movie, "The Wizard of Oz," where Dorothy and her friends are standing before the Wizard? He's making big noises, and shooting off fire, and scaring them silly. Just then, Toto tugs on a curtain off to one side, and reveals a rotund little man behind that curtain throwing switches and moving levers. At this point in the story, Oz thunders, "PAY NO ATTENTION TO THAT MAN BEHIND THE CURTAIN!!!"

The insurance claims process is a lot like that. The companies don't want their policyholders to question the claims procedure, or figure out that it can work very differently from the way that it looks. Insurance companies and claims adjusters want policyholders and claimants to be compliant and trusting. That decreases the size of the settlements, and increases the profits of the insurance companies.

**I'm going to be your "Toto."** In this book, and at my website, I'm going to pull back the curtain and show you how things really work. I'll show you how you can take control of your insurance claims and your policies, and add hundreds...even many thousands of dollars...to your insurance claim settlements. These are dollars that you are ALREADY entitled to collect from your policy.

In addition to the "how-to" parts of the book, I'm going to include some stories of commercial claims I've actually handled over the years. They're stranger than fiction...some are kind of gruesome...and all true.

Dorothy had a little dog and three friends that helped her get to the Land of Oz. That was her team. Let's stop for a minute and think about teams.

I started playing baseball on the Pee Wee League team in Kent City, Michigan, in the summer of 1962. I was 8 years old. I was always a second string first baseman, because my cousin Thomas was better than me at everything...hitting, running, fielding. All of the kids on that team were from that little village of about 600 people in West Michigan, and we had been playing together since kindergarten.

We won the league championship that year...and the same boys kept playing together as we got older. Our coaches were Don Kik and Pete Imkamp, and they administered discipline and love in equal doses to a bunch of small town boys.

We won every championship every summer until I was 14…Pee Wee League, Little League, Pony League, Junior Varsity. The summer I turned 14, we moved to a bigger town (a whopping 2,500 people) where my Dad had a construction business. As a sophomore in the spring of 1969, I finally became a starting first baseman. I played on the Junior Varsity at school, and that team won the conference championship.

I never knew what it was like to play on a baseball team that was not the champion. But remember, I wasn't the star on any of those teams. I was an average player on a championship team.

But I still got to share in the glory…just like a star.

Have you ever been on a sports team? Did you play Little League baseball, or Youth Soccer, or football, or basketball? If you did, you know how important it is to have great players on your team.

You also probably remember how painful it was when your team lost.

**Friends, the stakes are way too high when it comes to handling an insurance claim.**

You cannot afford to have your team lose now.

When it comes to your insurance coverage…no matter what kind of insurance…you need to have a team. But…

WHO DO YOU HAVE ON YOUR TEAM?

The insurance company has trained adjusters who are experts in the claims process.

ANYONE LIKE THAT ON YOUR TEAM?

The insurance company has well trained claims examiners who are experts on reading and interpreting YOUR insurance contract.

ANYONE LIKE THAT ON YOUR TEAM?

The insurance company has staff attorneys that can answer their questions if a legal issue comes up in your claim. The company will hire the best trial lawyers money can buy to defend the insurance company in court if your claim goes to trial.

ANYONE LIKE THAT ON YOUR TEAM?

The insurance company has Training and Compliance experts to make sure that the claim is handled correctly, and according to the state statutes where the loss occurred.

ANYONE LIKE THAT ON YOUR TEAM?

The insurance company has forensic engineers at its disposal, who will make engineering inspections and write reports for them.

ANYONE LIKE THAT ON YOUR TEAM?

The insurance company has forensic accountants at its disposal. These are accounting experts who can evaluate a complicated loss, like a luxury home or a business income loss.

ANYONE LIKE THAT ON YOUR TEAM?

The insurance company has personal property replacement companies at its disposal. These companies give super low prices to insurance companies on everything from automobiles to electronics to jewelry, and everything in between. You'll probably have to pay retail.

ANYONE LIKE THAT ON YOUR TEAM?

The insurance company has salvage companies at its disposal, in order to take damaged goods and sell them, thereby recovering some of the money the insurance company paid in your claim.

ANYONE LIKE THAT ON YOUR TEAM?

The insurance company has private investigators at its disposal. These people will perform background checks, neighborhood interviews, public records searches, even conduct surveillance of YOU at home and at work.

ANYONE LIKE THAT ON YOUR TEAM?

DO YOU EVEN <u>HAVE</u> A TEAM?

DO YOU THINK THAT YOU MAY BE AT A HUGE DISADVANTAGE?

<u>Keep reading…your disadvantage is just about to disappear!!!</u>

\* \* \* \* \*

Far and away the greatest satisfaction comes to me when my strategies help people recover thousands more dollars in their claim settlements! That is why I published the first book in 2007.

But now that this book on commercial claims is published, my level of satisfaction is going to grow exponentially!

**<u>This entire book is about helping YOU, THE POLICYHOLDER OR CLAIMANT, maximize the amount of money you are entitled to receive from the insurance company when you have a loss.</u>**

I can't possibly help more than a few hundred people in a year. I'm only one guy in one place. However, with this book, millions around the globe will be helped getting their claims paid.

Deepak Chopra says that one of the most important things we can do for ourselves is to turn our inner dialogue from the question "What's in it for me?" to "How can I help?"

This is my greatest motivation for writing this book. I can truly envision millions of people the world over reading this book and doing the simple things it shows. I envision those millions of people collecting untold millions of dollars that they would not have collected if it were not for the strategies in this book. I am eager to receive letters and emails from people all over the world, telling me how this book made a difference in their lives.

Perhaps one of those people who write to me will be you. I'm waiting to hear YOUR story.

My sincere thanks to:

Dr. Tim Ryles, former Georgia Insurance Commissioner. Tim was so very gracious to read my manuscript and make very important recommendations.

This book is dedicated to my Redhead, Julie. I made her a promise that I'd love her forever, and I'm keeping that promise. In all of my life, I've never known a more fascinating woman. I'm still amazed and thankful every day that she loves me. Thank you, Julie, for your loving patience and unflagging support. I love you.

Hey, Julie! I wrote another one! Who knew?

Finally, to all my readers around the globe – past, present and future. Thanks for such wonderful support. May your lives be enriched and restored, and may you achieve peace of mind and heart.

# FOREWORD

Here is the **DIRTIEST little secret** of the insurance claims business:

**Any claims adjuster can help the policyholder maximize their claim recovery. They don't have to be splashy about it. They don't have to tell the insurance company that they are helping increase claim amounts. They don't have to put anything special in their files or in their reports. All the adjuster has to do is explain the claims process to the policyholder and help them carefully document their claim.**

**Then, why don't they?**

The truth is that most adjusters adhere to the philosophy of helping the giant wealthy insurance company minimize claim amounts. That is the reason that I could write two books about insurance claims secrets that have been such hot sellers. That's also the reason that I can't get hired any more in the insurance claims business.

And the experiences you have already had with claims adjusters, or you may be experiencing RIGHT NOW are the reasons you bought this book. So, make it count! You will leave thousands, perhaps hundreds of thousands of dollars on the table if you do not use my strategies!

In one way, insurance is nothing more than promises made between two parties.

In another way, it is much, much more than that. It's legally binding contract.

The insurance company writes a policy that makes commitments to you…promises.

The insurance company expects you to pay a fee, called a premium. In the policy, there are things that both of you must do, which is your way of keeping your promises.

The agent who sells you a policy makes promises about how the policy will protect you. We all hope that those promises made by the agent are actually found in the policy!

When it is all said and done, the process of filing a claim, and getting that claim paid, is the way that the promise is kept. <u>It is the essence of the insurance contract.</u>

## <u>CLAIMS ARE ALL ABOUT KEEPING PROMISES.</u>

**Commercial Insurance Claim Secrets REVEALED!**

The reputation of an insurance company is usually not spoiled by charging high premiums, because few people complain if they're convinced that there's more value in the policy than the amount of money they pay.

The reputation of an insurance company is usually not spoiled by paying huge commissions to their agents, because most people couldn't care less how much money their agent makes.

The reputation of an insurance company is usually not spoiled by investing money poorly.

Reputations of insurance companies are usually ruined due to poor claims handling.

Insurance companies spend millions of dollars in advertising to convince you that you're better off or smarter to do business with them. They tell you how many people switched to their company last year. (They never say how many people left or got cancelled though) They want you to buy their policies and remain their customers for a long time. In the insurance business, that's called "persistency." Persistency means policies that stay on the books for a long time. Agents get bonus money when they have good persistency.

I considered it part of my job as an adjuster to make the insurance company and the agent look good. If I treated the policyholder with compassion and respect, and did everything I could to get their claim paid as soon as possible, I knew that the policyholder would think positively about the insurance company and the agent that sold them the policy. I even told the policyholders what a great agent and great insurance company they had...just so they wouldn't miss my point.

I did this quite selfishly...I freely admit it. If the agents were happy with the way I took care of their clients, they asked for me to be the adjuster whenever their policyholders had a claim.

I also know that the claims examiners at the insurance companies are human beings just like you and me. They love people who make their work easier, and don't love people who make their work harder. If I sent them good reports that contain all the information they need to pay a claim, they could pay the claim and close the file.

For a claims examiner, cleanliness is not what's next to godliness...a closed file is next to godliness!!

I was able to make the insured, the agent and the company happy while quietly maximizing claim amounts.

When a policyholder is my client, my priorities become the policyholder's interests exclusively. My job then is to help them collect the highest possible claim recovery under the terms and conditions of their insurance contract.

So, either way, I'm on the policyholder's side in a claim situation.

Another way that I've found to be on the side of the policyholder is to help them get good coverage. I built an insurance quote website at:

## www.InsuranceQuoteHQ.com

If you can get the best coverage for the lowest price, you will have found your best insurance value. But low price is not enough when you are considering insurance. Even having a great agent is not enough.

There are hundreds of websites where you can get insurance quotes. Some of them are good, some not so good. I have visited dozens and dozens of these websites, and I noticed a common flaw.

They don't think like a claims adjuster. They think like sales people.

The other quote websites seem to be all about the lowest cost insurance quotes. Now, don't get me wrong. I like low prices as much as the next guy.

But, isn't there usually a difference between lowest price and best value?

Insurance is a service, not really a product. So, great customer service should be near the top of your list of benefits for buying insurance.

But you should not be only concerned with great customer service when you're buying your policy.

You should be MOSTLY concerned with the service you get when you have a loss. After all, insurance is all about keeping promises.

You enter into a contract with the insurance company. You promise certain things, like paying your premium. They promise to pay your claim if your loss is covered.

But most people I've ever talked to don't know the first thing about how to handle an insurance claim. That puts them...YOU...entirely at the mercy of the insurance company and the insurance adjuster.

Many times, people who have had a loss are on the raw edge of emotion. Isn't is natural to be fearful in a situation where you don't feel you're in control...where you don't know what will happen next, and you're scared you'll be "ripped off?" Most everyone has heard a story from a relative or friend about an insurance claim that went badly.

People like that need solid advice and claim strategies on what to do to get their claim paid.

They need to understand the claims process completely so that they are not at the mercy of the insurance company, the claims adjuster and the claims examiner.

They need to be paid every dollar that they are entitled to collect.

They need to have peace of mind knowing that their claim was handled correctly.

Every policy you can buy will have a section that tells you what you must do when you have a loss and want to file a claim. But, the policy NEVER tells you HOW to file your claim. The policy NEVER tells you about the "claims process."

Why?

It's simple, really. If you don't know where to turn for help in the claims process, you will naturally turn to the insurance company's claims adjuster for help. If you allow them to help you prepare and submit your claim, you can be certain that you will NOT COLLECT every dollar you should. If the insurance company controls the claims process, YOU LOSE!

The "devil is in the details" of the claims process. The insurance companies all rely on the fact that their policyholders don't know the claims process. That lack of knowledge helps the insurance companies hold down claim settlement amounts. That increases their profits...but at your expense.

So, what can you do?

You must become at least as claims-conscious as price-conscious.

So, go ahead and confidently get the best insurance quote and lowest price on your insurance!

And I'll help you become claims-conscious! Here's how...

I recommend taking a four-step approach:

1. Use your computer browser and go to: www.InsuranceQuoteHQ.com. Click through at the nav button that best suits your needs and fill out the simple form so that we can get the insurance companies and agents competing for your insurance business. We provide multiple vendors for some insurance products so you have even more choice and more options. We recommend clicking through at more than one vendor so you can really compare pricing.

2. Compare the insurance quotes carefully and make sure that the quotes have the same coverage.

3. Buy the coverage you need at the most competitive rates.

4. Once you've completed the simple quote form and submitted it, come back to this website. Click on the SPECIAL REPORT nav button on the left of the page. When you leave your email address, I will instantly send you TWO SPECIAL REPORTS on buying Car Insurance:

  - "5 Things To Do When Buying Car Insurance" (a $9.95 value)

  - "5 Things To Avoid When Buying Car Insurance" (a $9.95 value)

You will not spend one single cent! They are my gift to you. The reports are available to anyone visiting this website with no cost or obligation. You can have 'em even if you don't get a quote!

**Insurance You Deserve in 3 Easy Steps!**

1. You complete one quick form

2. We match you with hungry providers

3. You pick the best one

Our service is FREE! There is no credit check and no obligation to purchase...EVER!

Privacy Policy: We NEVER share your email with ANYONE ELSE. PERIOD.

No other insurance quote site in the world can offer you this winning formula for getting the best insurance rates AND maximizing your insurance claim settlements! No matter if your claim is a homeowners, renters, auto, business, etc.......

**THESE STRATEGIES WORK EVERY TIME!**

**CHAPTER ONE**

# WHAT IS A CLAIMS CONSULTANT?

There are two areas of handling finances that can cost you a fortune. <u>And you control both of them</u>.

The first is taxation. Your tax liability is often larger than any other expenditure you make. Nothing you can do is as important as proper tax planning. You can save yourself thousands of dollars each year by proper tax planning. I always say, "I will pay every dollar I owe, but not a cent more than I owe."

For most people, they trust their tax planning to a tax professional, such as an accountant or tax attorney. Why? They know that a specialist can save them money far in excess of the fee the specialist charges.

The second area of handling finances is insurance claims. Few people are well versed in the claims process. The devil is in the details of the claims process. You also have a life to live or possibly a business to run during the time you work through the claim. You cannot abandon life and business to handle a claim.

An insured loss can be a frightening event.

A car wreck can be traumatic, with both property damage and personal injuries. You could also be subject to lawsuits.

A home or business fire turns your world upside down, and dealing with all the issues can be overwhelming.

A tornado or hurricane is even worse than a fire. Where do you turn when all your neighbors and the community are suffering too?

When a business has a major loss, the owners have to split their time between the claim and the very survival of the business. Many businesses do not survive a major insured loss.

Peace of mind flies away during times of high stress, and few things are as stressful as an insurance claim.

So, where do you go to get your questions answered when you're having trouble with your insurance claim?

If you have an insurance claim...even a small claim...you will benefit by enlisting the services of a claims consultant. He can help you collect every dollar you are entitled to collect. He is your personal insurance specialist...the head of your team.

Once you submit an insurance claim, you become the insurance company's adversary. You are making a financial claim against that company's assets. So, can you trust their advice?

When it comes to handling your insurance claim...whether it's a property or casualty insurance claim...you need to have your own claim support team.

When it comes to buying your insurance coverage…no matter what kind of insurance…you need to have your own support team.

The insurance company has their claims team that will do everything in their power to minimize, delay or deny your claim. Don't be misled by all the "fast claim settlement" ads. If you settle your claim fast, you gave them a discount whether you know it or not.

Ask yourself these three simple questions:

**1.** Do I have the expertise and experience necessary to handle my own claim?

**2.** Is the amount of the claim going to be large enough that I could lose hundreds or even thousands of dollars without a claims consultant to guide me through the claims maze?

**3.** Without a claims consultant, how will I know whether the insurance company settlement is fair, and enough money to return me to my pre-loss condition?

Your answers to those three simple questions will show you what you need to do.

"OK," you say. "I can see my huge disadvantage when I file a claim. I know I need a claims consultant of my own."

**"But where do I find a claims consultant who will be on my side and help me in my insurance claim?"**

How DO you find a claims consultant? I invite you to spend an hour searching the major Internet search engines for every keyword imaginable. If you can find another person who does what I do, please let me know. I'd love to know about him!

What you may find are some Public Adjusters using the title "claims consultant." But a PA doesn't usually accept a client on an hourly basis. (Some states do require PAs to charge hourly rates rather than a contingency fee.) A typical PA won't consult you on your automobile claim. A typical PA will not consult with you if your claim is small and they don't think they will make enough money for the time they invest.

So, where do you go when your claim is not a good fit for a PA?

**Look no further...here I am!!**

What about an attorney?

Personal Injury Attorneys handle claims for injured people all the time, but seldom handle property losses. Sometimes a personal injury attorney cannot help you because your settlement looks like it will be too small. And because most PI attorneys don't handle property losses, and they cannot tell you the insider claims strategies that I know. Finally, an attorney will want to represent you for a fee, not just advise you on how to handle your claim yourself.

So, where do you go when you need claims strategies but your claim is not a good fit for an attorney?

**Look no further...here I am!!**

I am a nationally-renowned claims consultant. In my claims consulting practice, I advise policyholders, claimants, Public Adjusters and attorneys in the submission of claims.

I will review your claim and make recommendations for the strategies you must use in your own individual claim to resolve disputed issues and settle the claim, adding hundreds or even thousands more dollars to your claim settlements.

I will consult with you on:

- Commercial insurance claims
- Automobile insurance claims
- Homeowners insurance claims
- Renters insurance claims
- Purchasing insurance policies and getting quotes

If you have any questions about any aspect of an insurance claim, I will answer your questions and give you the advice you need to complete your claim with the maximum settlement you are entitled to collect.

**HERE IS MY NO RISK, IRON-CLAD MONEY-BACK GUARANTEE:** My claim strategies will add hundreds or even thousands more dollars to your claim settlement. No matter how much you spend with me in claims consultant fees, if the additional amount of money you collect from the insurance company when you use my strategies does not exceed my fee, I will promptly refund every penny of my fee to you! But I have NEVER had a client ask for a refund.

Imagine the peace of mind you will feel knowing that you have a champion on your side, walking you through the claims process, helping you collect EVERY PENNY you are entitled to collect!

If we determine that you need assistance from an attorney or Public Adjuster, I can make recommendation of experts in your area, anywhere in North America. I can then assist your attorney or PA as needed.

If you are buying insurance and you want to get the best coverage for your money, I will customize your coverage requests so you'll get the best quotes and the best coverage.

## COMMERCIAL CLAIM CONSULTING

If you own a business and you have experienced a significant loss of any type, you may require individual consultations in person. I perform consultations in person anywhere on the globe. For more details, please contact me through the "Contact Us" nav button at my website to discuss fees, time schedule and any other issues.

## ATTORNEY CONSULTING

If you are an attorney that has clients who need claims strategies to help them maximize their claim settlement, you may retain me as a claim consultant to assist you with your client. Together, we can help your client collect every dollar they are entitled to collect. These strategies work every time, no matter if your client is a first-party policyholder or a third-party claimant.

### I Even Help Insurance Companies!!

Because of my expertise in claims adjusting, I am also able to help insurance companies in certain unusual, specialized cases. For example, I can help when a policyholder submits a wildly inflated claim for damages that exceed policy limits.

Recently, I completed a consulting project for an attorney who was representing an insurance company for a claim in which lawsuits had already been filed. The policyholder's buildings were submerged in the New Orleans flood after Hurricane Katrina, and suffered extensive damage. However, the policyholder's policy had sub-limits that restricted their recovery. The policyholder filed suit against the insurance company for their claim, which exceeded $16 Million. I was able to do a comprehensive analysis of the claim submitted by the policyholder and his attorney. In this incident, I was able to help the insurance company settle the claim for about $3 Million dollars. The insurance company saved over $13 Million dollars!

Please call or contact me through the "Contact Us" nav button at my website: http://www.insurance-claim-secrets.com .

CHAPTER TWO

# COMMERCIAL PACKAGE POLICY

I'm beginning the book with a very short chapter on the most popular form of business insurance...the Commercial Package Policy. These packages were first developed back in the 1970s and have become the most popular way for small and medium-sized business to get the coverage they need without buying a bunch of individual policies and trying to keep track of them.

Commercial Package Policies are insurance policies that combine property coverage with liability coverage. They are also known as the Business Owners Policy (BOP).

The CPP has been likened to being a Homeowner's policy for a business. Most of the coverages that are needed by small and medium-sized businesses are typically included. The major exceptions are Auto, Workers Compensation and Professional Liability. By combining coverages into one policy, business owners can save money on premiums and prevent administrative headaches.

Large businesses may have different needs for coverage than typically found in the CPP. Sometimes, the larger firm will simply need higher policy limits than are found in Package policies. Large companies frequently buy individual policies rather than package policies. Many times, large companies can write their own coverages, a product known as a Manuscript Policy. Instead of buying a policy written by the insurance company, the large companies will have underwriters draft their own coverages, and then go out into the insurance marketplace to find a company that wants their business.

The CPP is comprised of property coverage on Buildings and Business Personal Property, liability coverage and some optional coverages that can be added to the policy. A CPP will typically include:

Property Insurance, covering buildings, equipment and inventory (discussed in detail in Chapter Two)

Business Interruption and Extra Expense insurance (discussed in detail in Chapter Three)

Liability coverage, protecting the business from damage done by employees or products to others, as well as accidents and other coverages (discussed in detail in Chapter Six)

Crime Insurance, including burglary, theft and robbery, as well as employee theft and embezzlement

Vehicle coverage for rented or borrowed vehicles.

Many other coverages, such as Business Auto, Flood Insurance, Earthquake Insurance and some special liability coverage may be added to the CPP as endorsements.

The Commercial Package Policy is one of the best products ever designed by the insurance industry. In subsequent chapters, we will look more closely at coverages and how they affect you as a commercial entity.

CHAPTER THREE

# BUSINESS INCOME AND EXTRA EXPENSE

Business Income and Extra Expense (BI/EE) coverage are essential coverages for any commercial entity. The coverage is known by many names...Business Interruption Insurance, Loss of Use, Time Element...but they all mean basically the same coverage.

It's not just businesses that need BI/EE coverage. Any commercial entity that has cash flow and an income has a need to protect that income. That's why the BI/EE coverages are chosen as necessary coverages.

Businesses and commercial entities are primarily concerned with the real estate and personal property protection found in the Commercial Property Coverage Form CP 0010. But many times, the very survival of the business or commercial entity will rely upon loss of income protection. For this chapter, we're going to lump all of them together in the term "business."

## Business Income

Here are just a few examples of the need for BI coverage:

1. Refinery operation has a fire. All three shifts of work cancelled indefinitely. The business will be closed for a year due to the repairs. Building insurance is adequate, but without BI/EE the refinery could not survive without income for a year.

2. Insured manufacturer's facility hit by a tornado. Heavy building damage, most inventory damaged by rainwater. Manufacturer makes a crucial component of a finished product produced by a larger manufacturer 100 miles away. The larger manufacturer has to shut down assembly and production because they cannot get the components from the damaged business. They make a claim against the insured, which is called a Contingent Business Income loss.

3. Restaurant has a kitchen fire. Health Department shuts them down until repairs are completed, which will take three months. Owner won't be able to reopen without BI.

4. Owner of a 20-story office tower has a main sprinkler pipe burst on the 20th floor, flooding all 20 floors below and causing damage to all tenants. The occupancy rate is 75%. Rents vanish overnight as tenants move out. It will take a year to make repairs. Without BI, the landlord would default on his mortgage and the bank would foreclose on the property.

5. Spring floods overrun a huge grain elevator operation. Millions of tons of grain are contaminated by floodwaters. The operation has insurance for the buildings and inventory, but more inventory won't be available until harvest in the fall. BI loss.

6. 40-story luxury hotel struck by tornado. The hotel is a 600-room round tower, and every room has an exterior window wall. 350 window walls are blown out or damaged. The hotel was built in 1990, and the bronze-tint custom window walls must be manufactured especially for this hotel in order to match the tint of the remaining windows. The hotel cannot rent 350 rooms for a year. This also affects restaurant, catering, convention and gift shop revenues for a year. The hotel would be out of business in three months without BI.

7. As the final example, think about your own business. If you had a major loss that interrupts your business, how will you continue your business? No matter what type of business you operate, when the cash flow is delayed or stopped altogether, you are instantly in a crisis. Without Business Income insurance, the crisis could quickly kill your business.

Business Income protection has been designed to provide the business with "the actual loss of income sustained due to the necessary suspension of operations during the period of restoration. The suspension must occur within the policy period, and must be caused by direct physical loss or damage to property at the premises which are described in the policy Declarations"(actual policy language).

The definition of "Business Income" in the policy is "the net income (net profit or loss before income taxes) that would have been earned or incurred: and continuing operating expenses incurred, including payroll."

The BI loss is calculated one of two ways: gross profit less non-continuing expenses, or net profit plus continuing expenses.

## BI Strategies

Insurance companies expect their commercial claims adjusters to know how to calculate a BI loss. Most commercial claims adjusters do not know how to calculate a BI loss, even if it is a small one. Even if an adjuster does know the procedure of figuring out a BI loss, he knows that this procedure is an accounting process, not an adjusting process. Most adjusters are not accountants. Therefore, insurers hire Forensic Accounting firms, whose task is to evaluate the Business Income loss and write a report that states how much the policy should pay the insured. The insurance companies also know that, in a BI dispute that lands in court, the Forensic Accounting firm can be an expert witness. The adjuster usually does not qualify as an expert witness.

Now, compare this situation with your business tax preparation. Do you allow the IRS to calculate your tax liability? Even if you could allow the IRS to do your taxes, would you truly expect them to calculate your taxes at the lowest possible amount due?

No. That would be preposterous! Then don't trust your insurance company to calculate your BI claim for you. The insurance company is in the business of minimizing claims.

So, the most important BI strategy is to retain a Forensic Accountant or Public Adjuster of your own to prepare your BI claim for you. This one strategy could mean the difference of tens of thousands, perhaps hundreds of thousands of dollars that you may be entitled to collect.

## Extra Expense

Extra Expense means "the necessary expenses you incur during the period or restoration that you would not have incurred if there had been no direct physical loss or damage to property caused by or resulting from a Covered Cause of Loss (also policy language).

EE coverage pays to "avoid or minimize the "suspension" of the business and to continue operations at the described premises or at replacement premises or temporary locations, including relocation expenses and costs to equip and operate the replacement location or temporary location."

Under "Loss Determination," the policy states:

"The amount of Extra Expense will be determined based on:
1.) All expenses that exceed the normal operating expenses that would have been incurred by operations during the period of restoration if no direct physical loss or damage had occurred. We will deduct from the total of such expenses;
(a) The salvage value that remains of any property bought for temporary use during the period of restoration, once operations are resumed: and
(b) Any extra expense that is paid for my other insurance, except for insurance that is written subject to the same plan, terms, conditions and provisions as this insurance."

Here are just a few examples of the need for EE coverage:

1. Large private school struck by hurricane one week before school starts in September. School must find alternate locations immediately to keep the school operating and tuition payments coming from parents. Alternate locations are expensive as well as emergency purchases of books, supplies, etc. The school will take nine months to rebuild and repair.

2. Manufacturer has a fire loss, and their number one machine is damaged. They find another machine that can be shipped in, and production can resume more quickly. Express shipping will cost $50,000. EE pays the bill.

3. Water loss in a restaurant. Owner uses his own employees to make repairs instead of laying them off. The wages are covered by EE.

4. Business has a fire. They relocate to another building nearby to continue operations until the damaged building can be repaired. Relocation expenses are covered by EE.

## EE strategies

This is pretty broad coverage, and the determination of what are Extra Expenses is open to debate and always subject to negotiation.

The insurer and insured have opposing interests in the settlement of any claim. The insurer wants to calculate and pay the least amount, and the policyholder's interest are best served by maximizing the claim amount.

I encourage policyholders to retain their own forensic accountant or Public Adjuster to calculate and negotiate their BI/EE claim.

Hiring a Public Adjuster makes it possible for the insured and his employees to focus on keeping the business operating, and not taking time away from business survival to be working on the claim.

## Additional Coverages

A. Civil Authority

The policy pays for the actual loss of Business Income you sustain, and necessary Extra Expense caused by action of civil authority that prohibits access to the described premises due to direct physical loss of or damage to property, other than at the described premises, caused by or resulting from any Covered Cause of Loss. The coverage will begin 72 hours after the civil action and continue for a maximum of three consecutive weeks. The coverage for Extra Expense begins immediately after the civil action and will end three consecutive weeks later, or when the BI coverage ends, whichever is later.

For example, your business is located in an industrial park. A large chemical plant in the industrial park has an explosion that causes a large chemical cloud. Police and fire evacuate the area, including your business. The chemical cloud settles on the industrial park and a contamination quarantine is issued by the Health Department. No one goes into that area for 19 days. Contamination is cleaned up by the EPA contractors, and the quarantine is lifted. In this example, your BI loss would begin on the fourth day, but your Extra Expense would begin immediately after the evacuation. You would be paid for 16 days of Business Income and 19 days of Extra Expense.

B. Alteration and New Buildings

Coverage pays for BI and EE you sustain from damage to new buildings (complete or under construction), alterations to existing structures, and machinery and supplies located within 100 feet of the premises used in the construction and incidental to the occupancy of the building.

For example, you are building a new wing on your manufacturing building. You were two weeks from completion and moving all the new machinery into the building. During construction, a hurricane strikes. It will now take you another six months to repair and complete the building. The policy pays the BI and EE loss from the date that operations would have begun until operations actually begin.

C. Extended Business Income (other than rental value).

The policy pays the BI loss, beginning on the date that the property is actually repaired, and ends on the earlier of (1) the date you would generate the business income you had if no loss had occurred, or (2) 30 consecutive days after repairs are completed. However, this coverage does not apply to an income loss due to unfavorable business conditions in the area caused by the impact of the cause of loss.

This coverage differs from the primary BI coverage, which ends when your property is repaired. This extends coverage, at most, another 30 days after repairs are completed to allow you to get your business back to pre-loss production.

D. Interruption of Computer Operations

For example, a violent thunderstorm passes over your tool and die business and lightning strikes your building directly, causing a fire and severely damaging all electronics and electrical equipment. Not only are all your computers destroyed, but the computers that operate the CNC machines and lathes are destroyed also. You are out of business until all the electrical equipment and computers are replaced and reprogrammed. This extends coverage for the computer losses, but is based upon the Cause of Loss form your policy has.

The coverage also includes damage from viruses introduced into the computer meant to harm or disrupt operations. The coverage limit for this extension is $2,500 per year.

Another Coverage Extension - if a Coinsurance percentage of 50% or more is shown on the Declarations page, this BI and EE extends to property at any location you acquire other than fairs or exhibitions. The most it will pay is $100,000 at each location. This coverage extension is like a 30-day "gap" policy, to protect you during the first 30 days after acquiring a property. It expires if you report the new property within that 30-day period, or if the underlying policy expired before the gap closed.

Don't ever place your business in jeopardy of going out of business simply because you did not purchase Business Income and Extra Expense coverage. Protect your legacy and buy BI/EE coverage.

CHAPTER FOUR

# BUSINESS AUTO CLAIMS

You can usually add Business Auto coverage to any Commercial Package Policy. This type of Commercial Form provides coverage for business vehicles regardless of whether they are owned, leased, hired, or borrowed.

You need Business Auto or Commercial Auto coverage if you or any employees are using their vehicles while working. Some owners of small business believe that if their vehicle is titled in their name, they do not need Commercial Auto coverage. This is not true. The personal auto policy specifically excludes coverage for business use.

Don't waste time arguing with your insurance company if you have a collision loss while you are using your personal car to go on a sales call. If your personal insurance company finds out that you were working at the time of the accident, it will deny your claim.

. The Business Auto Form's coverages are divided into the following sections:

**1.** Section I-covers vehicles that are identified according to any one of nine symbols:

a. Symbol #1-any vehicle

b. Symbol #2-owned vehicle only

c. Symbol #3-owned private passenger vehicles only

d. Symbol #4-owned vehicles other than private passenger vehicles

e. Symbol #5-owned vehicles subject to no-fault insurance

f. Symbol #6-owned vehicle subject to compulsory uninsured motorists laws

g. Symbol #7-specifically described vehicles (only those listed are covered)

h. Symbol #8-hired vehicles only

i. Symbol #9-non-owned vehicles only

By using the symbols above, the business owner may select only the coverages desired, thereby minimizing its insurance costs. For example, if the business desired the most comprehensive coverage, he would select symbol #1.

**2.** Section II-liability coverage in the event the business' negligent acts and/or omissions result in bodily injury or property damage to a third party as the result of operating a vehicle.

**3.** Section III-physical damage coverage for property damage to the business' covered vehicles under three classifications:

a. Other Than Collision (OTC)-pays for all physical damage to the business' vehicles regardless of cause with the exception of collision with another object or in the event the vehicle overturns.

b. Specified causes of loss coverage-pays for physical damage to the business' vehicle only resulting from fire, lightning, explosion, theft, windstorm, hail, earthquake, flood, mischief, or vandalism; or sinking, burning, collision, or derailment of any conveyance transporting the business' vehicle.

c. Collision-pays for physical damage to the business' vehicle resulting from contact with another object.

**4.** Section IV-conditions that describe the insured business and the insurance company's obligations if a loss should occur.

**5.** Section V-definitions discussing the critical terms in the vehicle form such as the meanings of accident, insured, vehicle, or suit.

Now, were going to discuss claim strategies for your Business Autos. Not only do you need to understand these strategies, but you must also make these strategies clear to any employee that operates one of your vehicles. If you do not share these strategies with your employees, you risk losing your entire business. Your choice.

**I'm telling you these steps to protect YOU. Failure to do these steps could cost you hundreds of thousands of dollars or more in a judgment or settlement that goes against you.**

I've written many words and phrases in capital letters for emphasis, so you'll understand how crucial this information is. Yes, in "Netiquette" ('Net Etiquette) I'm hollering at you.

Here are the steps to take when you're in a traffic accident:

ON SCENE - <u>BEFORE YOU GET OUT OF YOUR VEHICLE OR TALK TO ANYONE!</u>

1. <u>**NEVER** </u>SAY IT WAS YOUR FAULT, **NEVER** ACCEPT BLAME OR ACCEPT LIABILITY...<u>NOT EVER...NEVER</u>.

2. AN APOLOGY IS AN ACCEPTANCE OF LIABILITY. UNDER NO CIRCUMSTANCES SHOULD YOU APOLOGIZE TO THE OTHER DRIVER, HIS PASSENGERS OR EVEN PASSENGERS IN YOUR OWN CAR. DON'T APOLOGIZE TO THE POLICE OFFICER, THE WRECKER DRIVER, THE AMBULANCE TECHNICIAN...NOBODY. Acknowledge that it happened...if you must say something, say you regret <u>that it happened</u>, cry if you must...but DON'T APOLOGIZE.

3. Make sure everyone in YOUR VEHICLE is OK. Find out if you or your passengers are injured. Once you take care of those in YOUR VEHICLE, then you could see about the other car(s).

4. If you can, call the police and report your accident and injuries.

5. If it is possible, and your vehicle is still operable, move it out of the active roadway and off to the shoulder of the road.

6. If it's not possible to move your car, get yourself and your passengers to a safe place, such as the side of the road, out of the traffic lanes. If it is too dangerous to cross active lanes of traffic to get to safety, STAY INSIDE THE CAR.

7. Get your driver's license, vehicle registration and proof of insurance out, ready to present them to the police officer.

8. When the officer arrives on the scene, be cooperative, but don't volunteer information. If the officer asks you if you are at fault, I recommend that you tell him you do not know. That is an entirely true statement. You are not the person or court of law that would determine who is at fault. Neither is the police officer, even if somebody gets a ticket. You may think you're at fault, but may not be legally at fault. Even if you get a ticket, that does not necessarily prove that you are at fault. The law in some states has statutes of comparative negligence, which means you might only be found partially at fault, or not at all.

8. If you have a camera, or a cell phone with a camera, take as many photos as you can of:

a. The vehicles. If it's a multiple vehicle accident, you'll have a photo record of the description of each auto. Take shots of each license plate. Try to get photos before the cars are moved from the point of impact, if you can. If one vehicle is a commercial vehicle, like an 18-wheeler, take a photo of the writing on the driver's door.

b. The damages. I've seen claimants try to get paid for damages having nothing to do with the accident.

c. The accident scene. Crucial evidence at an accident scene can be destroyed quickly. Skid marks can wear off, or can wash off with the first rain.

d. The wrecker. I've seen wreckers send a bill to the insurance company for accidents they didn't work.

e. The other driver and passengers. That way, you'll know who was involved, how many were involved, what they look like, and maybe their injuries will show. I've seen claims where people swore they were passengers in one of the cars, and were not even there.

9. Don't argue with the police officer. If you get a ticket, just sign it and accept it. Your attorney can deal with it later, but at the roadside, you'll probably not be successful arguing about it.

10. DON'T SIGN ANYTHING ELSE AT THE ACCIDENT SCENE…NO MATTER WHO INSISTS ON GETTING YOUR SIGNATURE.

11. DON'T GIVE A RECORDED STATEMENT TO ANYONE AT THE ACCIDENT SCENE, NO MATTER WHO ASKS FOR IT. Tell them you'll give your statement in the presence of your attorney.

12. DON'T GIVE A WRITTEN STATEMENT AT THE ACCIDENT SCENE…NO MATTER WHO ASKS FOR IT. Tell them you'll give your statement in the presence of your attorney.

LATER, AFTER THE ACCIDENT.

1. Call your insurance company and notify them of your involvement in the accident. Make sure you notify them the way they require in the policy. Even if you are not at fault, you MUST notify YOUR insurance company. If you do not, you could be in violation of the terms of your insurance policy, and become ineligible for the insurance company to defend you in a lawsuit.

2. Call your Attorney. Tell the attorney the details of the accident. He can then advise you of the procedure you should undertake, and advise you of your legal rights. See Chapter Seventeen, "Should I Get a Lawyer?"

3. Read Chapters Twenty Nine, "Recorded Statements."

DO WHAT THESE CHAPTERS SAY TO DO!!

## SETTLEMENT TIPS

The insurance company and adjuster are going to try their best to pay you the lowest ACV price for your vehicle. They'll use the Kelly Blue Book, or the Black Book or some method of determining the value of your vehicle. But, there are a lot of variables to the value of a vehicle, like:

- you're meticulous, and detail your vehicle regularly. You only use the dealership for service, and you've kept all the receipts for services since you bought the vehicle. Your vehicle is worth more than an average vehicle.

- you had aftermarket customizing done to your vehicle...like custom paint, an auto wrap or some other advertising medium.

- you had a tailgate lift on your vehicle.

- your vehicle is a commercial truck and you had custom wheels, extra chrome, a custom sleeper, or any other accessories.

With just these variables, you can see that the average price for your make and model that goes through the local auto auction is not going to be acceptable to you. There could easily be hundreds of dollars of difference between what you KNOW your vehicle is worth, and what the insurance company and adjuster think it's worth.

IN CASES LIKE THIS...rely on your documentation and photos of your vehicle. You do have photos of your vehicle, don't you?

Or, what if you have an ordinary vehicle with average miles on it, and you still don't think that the adjuster is being fair with you on the amount of settlement?

Carefully document the make, model, mileage and condition of your vehicle. Go online and get a photo of what your vehicle looked like. Or, go to a dealership and find a vehicle that is as closely alike to yours as possible, and take a photo. Add in your Bill of Sale for your vehicle which shows what you paid for it.

Then take this file of information to three to five automobile or equipment dealers (I like five better), and ask to speak to the Manager. Make sure at least two of those dealers sell the make of your vehicle. For example, if your vehicle was a Freightliner, go see Freightliner dealers. Tell him you need a <u>written appraisal</u> of the vehicle based upon the information in the file.

Once you get that information you'll have a range of prices from lowest to highest. Start negotiating with the adjuster from the highest price. If he accepts your high price, fine. If he makes counter offers, come down on your offer in increments of $50.00 until you and he reach agreement.

Just remember, once you've made an offer, SHUT UP until the adjuster either accepts or makes a counter offer.

If nothing works, and you cannot come to agreement, send the insurance company a written certified letter invoking the Appraisal Clause in the policy. Each party chooses a competent appraiser, and the appraisers agree on an umpire. An agreement between any two will be binding, and you'll have your fairest price for your vehicle.

SURE, IT'S A LOT OF WORK…but don't you want to be SURE you are in charge, and don't you want the peace of mind to KNOW that NOBODY RIPPED YOU OFF?

You can do this, my friend!!

**CHAPTER FIVE**

# ALABAMA CELEBRATIONS

A few years back I received a claim assignment from a large commercial insurer. Their policyholder was a huge beer distributor in Birmingham, Alabama. The insured had filed a claim because he had roof leaks throughout the building. They thought that the roof leaks were due to a violent July thunderstorm that had passed through the area.

So, I called the insured. I found out that the building had been built about three years previously, and that it was a Butler™ pre-engineered building with the MR-24 standing seam roof. I had lots of experience with the MR-24, so I knew that this could be an expensive claim if it was a covered loss.

You see, the MR-24 roofing system is a floating metal panel roof system, and the seams between the 24-inch panels are crimped like the top of a soda can. So, making repairs to this type of roof is very difficult. Un-crimping panels is tough to do.

I made a second call to the biggest roofing contractor in Birmingham and asked him to meet me at the distributor's building so we could inspect the roof together.

So, I drove over to Birmingham from Atlanta and met with the owner and roofer. This building was big enough that it had interior ladders to roof hatches, so it was easy for us to get on the roof. Fortunately for me, the day I was there was a drizzly day, so we could see the places inside the building where the leaks were occurring.

When we got onto the roof, we found no wind damage, no hail damage...nothing that would explain the roof leaks. Then, almost by accident, we noticed some small holes in the metal roof panels. There were six of them, scattered around on the roof, near the roof leaks. The holes were about as big around as a pencil, maybe a little bigger. The holes appeared to be punctures.

The owner said that none of his employees had been on the roof in over two months. I was puzzled. What could have caused these holes in the roof panels?

"I'll tell you exactly what caused the holes," said the roofer. "They are bullet holes!'

"Bullet holes?" I replied.

"Exactly," he said. "Today is July 14th. We haven't had a rainstorm in Birmingham since before the 4th of July."

"The good ol' boys here in Alabama like to shoot their guns in the air on the big national holidays. The bullets go up in the air and have to come down somewhere. Lots of times, the bullets hit roofs and poke holes in the roof. We do a huge business in bullet-hole roof repairs in the 30-day periods after New Years Day, Memorial Day, the 4th of July and Labor Day."

Just amazing, isn't it? But was it covered?

Fortunately for the beer distributor, he had the Commercial Property Broad Form CP1020 policy, which provides coverage for the peril of Falling Objects. Bullets count as falling objects.

So, the owner got his very expensive repairs paid for by the insurance company...for falling bullets.

If you happen to be in Birmingham on a major holiday, I'd recommend staying indoors after dark.

<br/>

CHAPTER SIX

# COMPREHENSIVE GENERAL LIABILITY

We live in a very litigious society these days. Even small accidents and mistakes can result in large lawsuits. Some lawsuits are simply a nuisance that we must attend to. Others have significant financial risks. But all lawsuits must be defended. To protect themselves, businesses buy general liability insurance. General liability (GL) insurance protects the assets of a business when it is sued for something it did...or did not do...to cause injury or property damage.

You can purchase liability insurance as a stand-alone policy or as part of a Commercial Package Policy (CPP). A CPP combines property and casualty insurance into one policy. However, the liability limits in a CPP are customarily low. If your company needs higher liability limits, you may either add more coverage through a liability endorsement, or you can buy a separate policy.

You will calculate how much liability you need based upon a couple of factors:

- The state in which you are domiciled. Some states have a reputation and history of awarding high damage amounts to plaintiffs. You'd need higher liability limits in such a state.

- Your risks. You will evaluate the kinds of risks you face in your business. A company manufacturing firecrackers will have a greater risk of being sued than a company that manufactures fabric. A medical practice will need higher limits than a flower shop.

In a general liability policy, the insurance company will pay the legal costs of a business for a covered damage claim or lawsuit. Coverage includes claims for bodily injury, property damage, personal injury (different from bodily injury) and advertising injury. The policy covers general damages and compensatory damage. But many policies do not cover punitive damages, since they are considered punishment for intentional acts.

The GL policy provides coverage for individuals involved in your business such as:

- If your business is a partnership or joint venture, all partners or members and their spouses - but only for acts in a business capacity.

- If your business is a corporation or association, there is coverage for all executive officers, directors, and stockholders while acting in their business capacities.

- Employees are protected while acting in their capacity as

employees.

• Another subsidiary business for which you own more than 50% of the voting stock.

• A vendor, a person or any other entity with whom you have a written agreement to indemnify against liability claims arising from your work together.

• Newly acquired entities are customarily covered for up to 90 days.

• Your legal representatives are covered for any liability arising from the maintenance or use of property in their care, custody or control.

• Volunteers acting under your direction and within the scope of their responsibilities to you are covered.

A liability policy will sometimes have a single limit of liability to be paid during the policy period. Other policies will have a maximum liability per occurrence, with a maximum amount payable during the policy period.

For example, if a company has a $1 million policy limit, and has two lawsuits that award the plaintiffs a total of $1.1 million, the policyholder is responsible for paying $100,000.

Here are the coverages for a CGL or CPP policy:

• Bodily Injury - legal liability for injury, sickness, disease or death.

• Property Damage - legal liability for damage to the property of others, or loss of use of the property of others.

• Products and Completed Operations - coverage for claims against you for products your company made or services your company provided.

- Contractual Liability - legal liability that you assume when you enter into various contracts, such as a lease, a licensing agreement, an indemnity agreement or a maintenance agreement.

- Liquor Liability - covers your legal liability for a liquor-related accident. If your company sells, distributes, manufactures or serves alcoholic beverages, this coverage does not apply. But if you offer alcohol for free at the company picnic, and there was an alcohol-related incident, you're covered.

- Fire, Lightning or Explosion Damage - if the damage is caused by you, you have this coverage. Also, the coverage applies to other parts of the building you occupy that may sustain damage because of your negligence. For example, if you own a duplex office building and damage your neighbor's space due to your negligence, your liability coverage will cover the neighbor's damage.

- Hired Auto and Non-Owned Auto - when there are no vehicles titled in the business name, this coverage will meet contract requirements. Hired Auto coverage is like an umbrella for auto rental coverage, adding or replacing their liability coverage. You still must cover the rental car for physical damage. The vehicle must be rented in the company's name. Non-Owned Auto coverage protects your company if your company is sued for an accident involving an employee using his vehicle on company business. These coverages can be added as an endorsement if not part of the master policy.

- Legal Defense Costs - even if your company is not liable for a claim made against you, the claim or lawsuit must still be defended. You will have coverage for legal fees, court costs, and reasonable expenses you incur assisting in your own defense.

- Medical Payments - medical and funeral expenses are covered for persons accidentally injured by you, your employees or on your business premises.

- Personal Injury - is different from Medical Payments. This is coverage for slander or libel, violating a person's right of privacy, false arrest or detainment, malicious prosecution, or wrongful eviction.

- Advertising Injury - covers damage you cause in your advertising or promotion of your product or service. Covers slander or libel, violating a person's right of privacy, infringing on a copyright, title or slogan, and copying another company's advertising ideas or style.

- Employee Injuries - are not covered here, but are covered under your Workers Compensation policy.

### Umbrella Liability Coverage

To protect businesses from awards in excess of their policy's underlying limits, business regularly purchase Umbrella policies. An umbrella starts coverage where the underlying coverage ends. Umbrella policies also provide coverage for liabilities not covered in the Commercial Package Policy or the Comprehensive General Liability policy.

To qualify for an Umbrella policy, the insurance company will require you to maintain certain liability limits on your business and your Business Auto coverages.

### Liability Claims Strategies

The best claim strategy to protect yourself in a liability claim is to hire your own attorney to represent you. Yes, I know that the insurance company is going to provide you with legal representation. But whose interests are they protecting?

Think about this. You get whacked with a lawsuit and they have to defend it. They could pay $50,000...$100,000...$500,000...$1 million or more on your behalf. Whose money are they protecting?

What if their interests or not in your best interests?

I'm not suggesting that you go it alone. I am suggesting that you should have a voice at the table representing you and your interests apart from the legal counsel provided by the insurance company.

Your attorney, hired to represent your interests, can be an invaluable champion for you during the stressful days of lawsuit and liability defense. Don't shortchange yourself. You'll never be sorry that you protected yourself and your business.

## CHAPTER SEVEN

# EMPLOYMENT PRACTICES LIABILITY

Is Your Business At Risk For a Lawsuit?

Employment Practices Liability Insurance (EPLI) is insurance that helps protect you against claims from your employees that result from the general conduct of your business.

Are you, the business owner, more likely to be sued by an outsider or by an employee? The answer in most cases by a significant and growing margin...is an employee.

According to the Equal Employment Opportunity Commission, the average number of Employment Practices Liability cases filed per year is a staggering 80,000 cases. According to a recent study, the average payout on an employee-related claim is up over 30% to approximately $180,000.

This new wave of litigation is not limited to large corporations. Mid-sized and small businesses are being devastated by EPLI lawsuits. A recent case illustrates the problem.

A jury in Philadelphia decided in favor of a plaintiff who worked at a water treatment company with fifteen employees. The plaintiff was subjected to national origin slurs and sued. After deliberating for only a half hour, the jury awarded the plaintiff $200,000 in back pay, $100,000 for emotional distress, and $265,000 for the plaintiff's attorneys, for a total of $565,000.

Here are just a few other crazy employment-related settlements:

- A jury awarded $80.7 million to a UPS female supervisor who alleged a male supervisor poked her breast during an argument.

- A New York jury found that the NBA sexually discriminated when it failed to make a woman a regular season referee, awarding $100,000 in lost wages, and $8 million in punitive damages.

- State Farm Insurance settled a sex discrimination class action for $157 million.

- Mitsubishi settled two sexual harassment cases arising out of the same incidents for $45 million.

- Publix Supermarket announced an $81 million settlement of a sexual harassment lawsuit.

- Restaurant chain Denny's settled a class action lawsuit over racial discrimination for $54 million.

- Restaurant chain Cracker Barrel settled an EEOC lawsuit over racial discrimination for $8.7 million.

Here are only some of the ways that employees can file lawsuits against employers:

1. Wrongful termination of employment
2. Age discrimination
3. Failure to hire or promote
4. Breach of an implied employment contract
5. Negligent hiring or evaluation
6. Sexual or other workplace harassment
7. Retaliatory treatment
8. Infliction of emotional distress
9. Employment related misrepresentation
10. Violation of employment related laws
11. Adverse change in terms of employment
12. Wrongful reference (deprivation of career opportunity)
13. Failure to grant tenure
14. Invasion of privacy
15. Libel, slander or defamation

Businesses are being destroyed by employee lawsuits. The cost to employers includes defense costs and payment of damages. A business has to defend itself in a lawsuit whether or not there is ever a judgment awarded. It can cost thousands of dollars to simply respond to an EEOC charge without any lawsuit.

### How You Can Protect Your Business

The best way to protect your business is by creating an Employee Handbook.

Take the time to create employment policies and procedures for your company. The very act of researching and writing down your procedures will enable you to evaluate how you run your business. Once you have written procedures in place and you take care to enforce those procedures, you can better defend your company against employee allegations and lawsuits.

Define hiring processes, and create checklists for the entire hiring process to make sure all laws and procedures are followed.

Define the employee disciplinary and/or termination procedures.

Design a comprehensive Workplace Safety program for your business. Make it touch every aspect of your business...front office, back office, mailroom, manufacturing floor, fleet and delivery, sales force...don't leave anything or anyone out.

Once you have written the employee handbook, have your attorney review it before it is published.

Once it's published, meet with every employee, either individually or as a group, and go over the handbook in detail. Require each employee to sign off, indicating that they have received a copy and had the Employee Handbook explained to the employee.

Then, take care to strictly enforce the employment procedures in the law and in your Employee Handbook. That also means that you must train your management team to follow the Employee Handbook procedures.

Insist on an exit interview for every employee laid off or terminated. At that interview, review all issues and have the employee sign off, saying that the issues have been explained, regardless of whether the employee agrees or not.

You should strongly consider recording every exit interview, either on audio or video. Video is better. Even if an employee refuses to sign any documents at the exit interview, you have proof that you conducted a proper exit interview. You'd be glad you had that video tape if you got sued by that employee for wrongful termination or some other perceived injury.

Finally, every business or commercial entity should purchase Employment Practices Liability Insurance. EPLI policies typically cover claims of wrongful discharge, workplace harassment and discrimination. Key elements of coverage for an EPLI policy include defense costs for the business as well as coverage for claims and jury awards. Make sure that you choose high liability limits, because jury awards can be ridiculously high.

CHAPTER EIGHT

# INLAND MARINE

Inland Marine (IM) insurance indemnifies loss to moving or moveable property and is an outgrowth of Ocean Marine insurance.

Modern insurance began in the 1680s as ocean marine insurance, protecting the carrier (the guy who owned the ship) from liability for cargo he was transporting on the high seas. IM policies became known as "floaters," since the property they were protecting was, for the most part, floating.

The term "Inland Marine" came into being as the transportation of cargo began on inland lakes, rivers and canals. By the 20th century, it also included transportation of cargo over land.

IM policies began as liability policies, since the insured was accepting liability for the care, custody and control of another person's property for a limited period of time. That is called a "Bailee" interest. Bailees such as dry cleaners, motor carriers and warehouse operators all have this liability exposure. Bailees are liable for safeguarding the property of others as if it was their own. Property insured by IM coverage is usually one of the following:

- Held by a bailee for a limited time
- At a fixed location
- A moveable type of goods often at different locations
- Actually in transit

Inland Marine insurance has continued to grow and expand to include the following types of coverages, most with some element of transportation inherent in them:

- Accounts Receivable
- Bailee Customer's Goods
- Builder's Risk
- Communication Towers and Equipment
- Computer Coverage
- Contractor's Equipment
- Commercial Floaters
- Dealers
- Exhibitions
- Fine Arts
- Furriers
- Installation
- Jewelers
- Leased Property
- Mobile Medical Equipment
- Motor Truck Cargo
- Museums

- Musical Instruments
- Processing Risks
- Rigger's Liability
- Scheduled Property
- Transportation
- Trip Transit
- Valuable Papers
- Warehouse Legal

### Does your business need Inland Marine Insurance?

Well, it depends on the type of business that you own. Inland Marine can be a crucial coverage for protecting your business property.

Do you place tools and other valuable equipment in your car or truck each workday to do your job?

Do you place other valuables, including data, in your vehicle that you own or are responsible for their care, custody and control?

Do you store, clean, service or repair property that belongs to others?

Do you move the property of others from one location to another by a commercial vehicle?

Most commercial property policies limit or exclude your coverage on these types of insurable property. That's where Inland Marine policies are so valuable. IM policies allow you to buy the coverage you need for the specific risks you face.

You must understand that all IM policies are different, with different terminology and different coverages. It is crucial for you, the policyholder, to know what your policy states...what is covered and what is excluded.

So, the first strategy is...READ YOUR POLICY. Be sure what you are insuring. Be sure of the coverages and the exclusions in your policy.

I spent eleven months on a project handling Motor Truck Cargo losses for the London market. The policies had very cleverly worded clauses and many restrictions and exclusions on coverage. Most of the insureds had not read their policy when they filed their claims. Unfortunately, many claims were not covered by the policies they had purchased.

For example, many policies had Refrigeration Breakdown Floaters attached to the Motor Truck Cargo policies. But, in order to qualify for coverage, the insured had to show that he got the refrigeration unit inspected no more than every 30 days. Truckers sometimes forget that requirement, and the insurance companies denied many claims just on that one clause.

I had to be the guy that issued the denial letters. Denial letters are not fun for the adjuster and really unpopular with the insureds. If an insured gets a denial letter on a claim for a $100,000 load of seafood because he didn't get the reefer inspected, that trucker could easily be put out of business.

Next: Make sure your policy limits are adequate for your risk. For example, in Motor Truck Cargo, don't pick up loads worth $200,000 when your liability limits are only $100,000.

Next: Be sure that you have included all property in your policy schedule. It's normal for a business to add and delete equipment regularly. But some policies won't automatically insure newly acquired property. Also, if you do not delete equipment you no longer have, you could be paying premium on property you no longer own.

Next: When you file your claim, quickly provide the claims adjuster with the necessary documentation to prove your loss. Bills of Lading, shipping manifests, driver logbooks, receipts and maintenance records are just some of the types of documents you may have to provide.

Inland Marine coverage provides valuable protection for your property and liability for your property, and as you move and store the property of others.

## CHAPTER NINE

# WORKERS COMPENSATION

Perhaps someday I will write an entire book just about Workers Compensation (WC) Insurance. Many experts before me have already done so, and I'm reluctant to plow that ground again. But I do have some comments about WC that you should know.

If you have employees, you must carry Workers Compensation insurance. That is a statutory requirement in every state.

Workers Comp is a very flawed system in every state of the United States. It began with the lofty intentions of politicians in each state who enacted laws to protect injured workers and get them medical benefits and treatment for their injuries. But, like most laws enacted by politicians, there are unintended consequences. Further, business lobbies, insurance companies, trial lawyers and medical lobbyists contribute huge amounts of money to the politicians at both state and Federal levels. Injured workers are individuals for the most part, and don't have lobbyists.

Would it be too difficult for you to guess which side gets the political favors in Workers Compensation legislation?

Employers who carry WC insurance think that the system is stacked in favor of the workers. The workers think the system is stacked in favor of the employers. Both opinions are right in some respects.

You business is going to be rated for premiums based upon your loss experience. Higher number of injuries will get you higher premiums. Low injuries gets low premiums.

This should drive you to be safety conscious in all your work procedures. Design a safety program for your business and write it into the Employee Handbook. Then enforce it, for the sake of your workers and the sake of your assets. Well-run safety programs save businesses thousands of dollars in premiums, as well as thousands of dollars in lost employee productivity.

**CHAPTER TEN**

# RENTAL PROPERTY INSURANCE ISSUES

There are basically three types of business entities that rent real estate property to others:

- Individuals who own houses, apartments, condominiums or commercial property and rent them for income.
- Corporations who own houses, apartments, condominiums or commercial property and rent them for income.
- Commercial property management companies.

For these entities, it is crucial to get the insurance coverage right. It is also crucial to file your claim right. Screw up either or both of these activities, and you could commit financial mistakes from which you might never recover.

No matter which business entity you choose....individual, partnership, or corporation, you must do what you can to protect your assets. You should consult an attorney to determine the best business entity for you...the one that gives you the highest level of asset protection.

Assuming you already have the best business entity, let's begin with getting the proper coverage.

## Property Owner's Coverage

As property owner, you are going to be renting your real estate property to another person or business. That means you retain some responsibility for the property. Your rental or lease agreement might place some or all the responsibility for maintenance and upkeep on the tenant. But, no matter how much responsibility you can contractually transfer to the tenant (a Hold Harmless Clause), you still own the property.

That usually means you must insure the property, or at least insure the building and premises.

### Dwelling Coverage

Be aware that if you own a single family residence that you rent, you cannot buy a Homeowner's policy. The HO-3 requires that the owner live in the dwelling. If you presently own a Homeowners policy on that dwelling, understand that the insurance company will deny your claims when they learn you don't live there.

You must buy a Dwelling Fire policy or a Commercial Property policy to cover your rental property. Either policy can be expanded to include Building and Liability coverage.

## Condominium Coverage

If you own a condominium and live in it, you can buy a Condominium policy that is much like a Homeowners policy. Customarily, condo policies cover the structure, often including the interior walls and fixtures. If you own condominiums and rent them, you must buy Commercial Property insurance. You cannot rent a condo you own and insure it under a Condominium Policy. The commercial policy will cover the building and premises. The condo tenant will be just like an apartment tenant, and he will have to buy his own Contents insurance.

## Apartment Coverage

If you own an apartment building, you must buy Commercial Property insurance. It will cover the building and premises. It will not cover the personal property of the tenant. These policies may be expanded to include Building and Liability coverage. If you have other structures or amenities, such as tennis courts, parking lots, exercise rooms, or play areas for children, they can be insured also.

## Commercial Buildings Coverage

Commercial buildings can take any form, from manufacturing to warehouse or retail, churches, schools, hospitals or processing plants. Any building that is owned by one party and leased to another party would qualify as a commercial building.

Commercial Property policies do not usually cover the leaseholder improvements done by the tenant, such as interior walls, remodeling and equipment.

Foreclosure Dangers

These days, a lot of property owners who have underlying mortgages are in danger of foreclosure. The only thing I can think of that would be worse than losing your property in foreclosure would be to have an insured loss during foreclosure, only to find out your policy got cancelled.

Policies get cancelled regularly for lots of reasons like:

• Policyholder in financial trouble allows policy to lapse due to non-payment of premium.
• Lender should pay the property insurance premium from an escrow account, but forgets to make the payment.
• Lender should pay the property insurance premium from an escrow account, but the loan gets sold to another lender, and the new lender doesn't pay on time.

You could be in the middle of a foreclosure and not know that your policy got cancelled. Then, if you had a large property loss, there would be no coverage. If you had a large liability loss, there would be no coverage. Either claim could run into the millions. You would be ruined.

Banks and mortgage lenders have to deal with large numbers of foreclosed and repossessed properties, also known as REO (Real Estate Owned) properties. The borrower defaults on his loan, and there's no one to pay the insurance premium, and the policy gets cancelled.

In each of these examples, the property ends up without insurance coverage. Banks and mortgage companies do not like having loans on properties without insurance. If the property burns down, so does their equity.

There are insurance policies called "Forced-Placed Insurance" sold by companies that specialize in that form of coverage. The insurer makes a deal with the banks and mortgage companies that it will write a policy from the date of cancellation of the borrower's coverage, and into the future…as long as a premium is paid. The insurers take all these properties sight unseen, with no underwriting. Most of the time, the insurer will actually back-dates the forced-placed policy to the date when the other policy cancelled…even after a claim is filed.

You can imagine that this is very high risk business for those insurance companies. They don't get a chance to look at any property, no matter if it's a high-rise office building in the wealthiest part of town, or a low income apartment complex in the worst part of a major city. The insurers accept them all. But, because they accept this high risk business, they charge premiums that are two…three…four times as much as a standard premium.

The insurers have a remarkably low loss ratio, and makes enormous profits on this line of business.

So, if you are a property owner with insurance coverage premiums coming from an escrow account, and your policy gets cancelled for any reason, the bank will pay the premium for you and charge it to your escrow account. That is, as long as you have an escrow account, even while you are in foreclosure.

The BIG problem…the HUGE problem for YOU…the property owner…is that the bank only cares about THEIR MONEY. They don't care about you, the Business Personal Property of your business, your legal liability, or your Business Interruption loss. They usually only write the policy for <u>the unpaid balance of the loan</u>.

Lenders don't care about the replacement cost of your property. Forced-placed coverage usually only covers the outstanding loan balance on your mortgage. So, if you had a building worth $1,500,000, and a loan balance of $750,000, the lender would buy a policy for $750,000. The lender only cares about getting the loan paid off.

Your commercial package policy covers your liability. Lenders don't care about your liability exposure. They don't care if a delivery man falls on your property and sues you for six figures. Forced-placed coverage only covers the outstanding loan balance on your mortgage. There is no liability coverage.

Your commercial package policy covers your Business Personal Property. Lenders do not care about your contents. They don't care if everything you own is destroyed. Forced-placed coverage only covers the outstanding loan balance on your mortgage. There is no BPP coverage.

Your commercial package policy covers your Business Interruption exposures. Lenders do not care about the survival of your business. They don't care if everything you own is destroyed. Forced-placed coverage only covers the outstanding loan balance on your mortgage. There is no BI coverage.

Also remember that the LENDER owns the forced-placed policy on your property, not you. The settlement checks will go to them, or perhaps made payable to the lender and you. But they usually won't let you cash the check.

So, what do you do if this happens to YOU?

One of these scenarios will explain your situation:

1. You were negligent, and allowed your policy to lapse. It's not the lender's fault. The insurance company notifies the lender of the cancellation date. The lender forced-placed a policy for the loan balance. You have a claim.

What do you do? Very carefully follow the steps in this book to take control of your claim. Then, as soon as the claim is completed, buy your own policy and cancel the one the lender owns. Just make sure that you have coverage IN PLACE before you cancel the lender's policy.

2. The lender was negligent, and allowed your policy to lapse. Then, the lender force-placed a policy for the loan balance. You have a claim.

What do you do? ALERT!!!! Get an attorney involved IMMEDIATELY!! Don't wait!! Don't try to be a nice guy!!

Get your documentation in order. Make sure that you can prove it was the lender's fault that the premium was not paid. Next, have your attorney call the person at the lender who manages the Escrow Department. Explain what happened, and ask them what they plan to do to make things right. If they fix the problem and you don't suffer any loss from their negligence, then all will be well.

How does the lender fix the problem THEY created?

The bank could contact your insurance company and accept liability. Many times, the insurance company will allow the bank to make the premium payment and reinstate the policy. Once that's completed, you can proceed with your claim based upon the insurance policy that you did have before the cancellation.

The lender could accept liability and pay your claim out of their own pocket. You'll usually see donkeys flying around outside your house right before this happens.

If the insurance company will not allow the policy to be reinstated, then you must seek damages from the lender itself. Your attorney must file a lawsuit against the lender.

### Watch this carefully!!

1. If you have an escrow account through your mortgage lender, make sure that your commercial insurance policy is in force at all times.

2. Call your commercial insurance company, and make sure that they are sending renewal notices and premium notices to you, not just your mortgage company. Too many mistakes happen too frequently to trust your mortgage lender to take care of your business.

So, you cannot afford to place all your assets and your property at risk by trusting someone else to handle your money for you. You cannot just pay your monthly mortgage payment and forget it.

**The strategy is to make CERTAIN that your escrow account keeps your commercial property insurance policy in force AT ALL TIMES!**

This strategy ALONE could save you, the owner of rental property, hundreds of thousands, perhaps many millions of dollars of insurance benefits.

**Final thoughts about foreclosure dangers!**   Your mortgage contract probably states that the mortgage company will replace your coverage in the event of the cancellation of your insurance coverage. However, if the mortgage company force-places an inferior policy, a true "replacement" of coverage has not occurred. Point this out to your attorney. You might have a very compelling cause of action against the mortgage company!!

Deductibles

When purchasing your policy, choose the highest deductible your finances will allow. You will save premium dollars. Place the equivalent of one deductible in a savings account against that terrible day that you need it.

Coinsurance

Beware of the coinsurance clause found in most commercial property policies. Make sure that your property is insured to value. Even if your policy would allow you to recover with a coinsurance value less than 100%, you still need to be insured to value in order to recover your entire loss amount.

## Property Owner's Liability

"Why buy liability coverage on my commercial rental property? I just own the building... I don't occupy the building. I'm not running the business."

You are the owner of the property. Your property could cause injury to others, or you could be found legally liable for injury to others, due to your negligence. Liability insurance covers your legal liability when you are liable, and also when you are not liable. The policy still provides you a legal defense when you are found not liable.

<u>Claims Against Property Owners</u>

When claimants make a claim, or file a lawsuit, they often use these strategies:

1. The deepest pockets strategy. The claimant/plaintiff will go after the entity with the most assets. That might be you as the property owner.

2. The fishing net strategy. When someone files a claim or a lawsuit, they will draw in everyone that could have an interest or could be found to be liable. What if the tenant allows his insurance to lapse, and there is a claim? The plaintiff will also come after you.

Therefore, you have liability exposures on your rental properties whether you know it or not. Your rental agreement or lease may have a "Hold Harmless Clause," in which the tenant protects the property owner from liability. But Hold Harmless agreements are penetrated or nullified in court all the time. You cannot afford to be exposed to this risk.

Get the right coverage. Be sure that your policy is the correct type of policy for your exposures.

## File the claim

Remember I said that you must get your coverage correct, and file your claim correctly, in order to prevent financial mistakes from which you could never recover. Follow the strategies found in the other chapters of this book to be certain that your claim is handled in a manner that maximizes your recovery.

**CHAPTER ELEVEN**

# THE PRINCE'S ROLLING THRONE

In the summer of 2008, my client was Lloyd's of London on a Commercial Trucking loss. The insured was a fellow whose first name was Prince, who was born and raised in Ghana, West Africa. Prince spoke English, but had such a thick accent that he was hard to understand.

Prince had a 1999 Freightliner conventional tractor with a sleeper unit and a 53' dry box trailer. Prince was en route from Miami to Atlanta hauling a load of auto parts. He was driving up the Florida Turnpike going north when he tried to pass another tractor-trailer and struck the other trailer in the rear. He messed up the front of his tractor pretty good, and a wrecker service hauled his tractor back to their impound yard.

The owners of the wrecker company took an immediate dislike to Prince. They refused to allow him to gain access to his truck, where his daily medication was stored. They also refused to release the truck to the body shop until we paid the towing bill, which was a staggering $20,000. So, I called the Sheriff's Department and spoke to the Captain. Then, I called the wrecker owner. I told her that if she did not allow Prince access to his truck right away, I would have her arrested and thrown in jail. Twenty minutes later, a Sheriff's deputy walked into her office with a set of handcuffs, and asked her what she wanted to do.

Prince got access to his truck to retrieve his personal effects right then.

I called a heavy equipment appraiser in Palm Beach, who went to the wrecker yard to inspect the truck. While he was there looking at the truck, he called me.

"There's a big problem, Russ," he said. "The truck is full of sh\*\*."

"What do you mean?"

"Seems that Prince didn't like to stop at truck stops to relieve himself," he replied. "So, he had a five gallon bucket with a snap-on lid, and he used that to do his business. When he struck that other trailer in the rear, the bucket rolled forward out of the sleeper and broke open. That spilled the contents of the bucket all over the inside of his truck. Looks like His Royal Highness had been storing up waste for quite a while."

So, I told the appraiser to write two appraisals...one for the collision damage, and one of the interior cleanup. The collision damage was about $10,000, and the cleanup cost about $5,000. We actually had to find an environmental cleaning company to do the work on the interior of the truck. No one from the wrecker company or the body shop would go near the truck until the truck had been cleaned.

The insurance company wanted to deny his environmental damages. But, I pointed out to them that the policy language did not exclude this damage, so that they were obligated to cover it.

Meanwhile, Prince had no money and no credit. He was sleeping in a homeless shelter at night while his truck was being repaired. He would call me on a pay phone and wail loudly about his situation. Unfortunately, I couldn't understand most of what he said.

The body shop had to order a new front end assembly for the tractor, which took a month to get delivered and installed. We paid the body shop and poop cleaners directly, and Prince drove his truck back to his home in Nevada. He must have found some money somewhere.

I wonder if he picked up a new five-gallon bucket along the way.

**CHAPTER TWELVE**

# DON'T BE IN A HURRY
## Or, "Don't Get Your Panties In A Wad"

This chapter will show you what to do in the first few hours and days after your loss occurs. There are some <u>crucial tips</u> below about keeping records, and hiring restoration contractors…don't miss them.

How many times have you heard an insurance company's radio or television commercial say how fast they settle claims? That really sounds good, doesn't it? Who wouldn't want their claim settled quickly?

But my experience has been that hastily settled claims are settled far below what they are worth. It's almost as if the policyholder or claimant becomes willing to give the insurance companies a big discount in return for the speed of getting a settlement check.

Don't be one of those people who are motivated by a quick settlement check.

I'm not suggesting that you should drag your feet and be uncooperative in the process. You should be very cooperative...<u>but on your own terms, not the insurance company's terms.</u> I'm saying that if you are in control of the claims process like you should be, it will not usually be speedy.

The process will move along in a businesslike manner, but you must not allow yourself to be rushed into a settlement. Even if the insurance company sends you a check before you're ready to settle, you're not required to cash it.

Let's look at the first 24-48 hours after you have a loss. It really does not matter if your loss is small or large or a jumbo catastrophic disaster. It does not matter if your loss is a property loss...like a hurricane or tornado or fire, or a casualty loss...like an automobile accident. There are some things that you must do to protect yourself, your business and your property.

## FIRE OR CATASTROPIC WINDSTORM (HURRICANE/TORNADO) CLAIMS

### FIRST THING TO DO IS TO CONTROL THE SITUATION

1. Make sure everyone is safe and accounted for...including the pets. Yes, business owners have pets at the shop.

2. Get medical attention for anyone on the premises that needs it...including the pets.

3. Contact your public utility companies. Have them send out a technician to shut off the water, power and gas immediately. That itself will increase the safety factor in your damaged building.

Speak with the Fire Marshall and the local Building Inspector regarding the safety of the building. You want to be sure it's safe for you to enter the building after the loss. There can be danger of collapse after substantial damage. If it is not safe, don't go in there…no matter what. You can replace STUFF, but you cannot replace YOURSELF.

AFTER THE UTILITIES ARE SHUT OFF, AND BEFORE THE RESTORATION COMPANY BOARDS UP THE Building…SAFELY do the next step.

4. Camera work

Get hold of a video camera and a couple of video tapes. You might need a floodlight or other very powerful battery-powered light. If your building is safe to walk through, take video footage of every room in the house where there is damage. Take footage from every angle in every room. Make sure you take footage of your damaged contents. Shoot footage inside closets…in open drawers, inside boxes, on bookshelves, inside cabinets, anywhere lots of personal property is stored. Take shots of all four sides of your building from the outside. Take footage of the debris on the property, especially if it has contents items that the fire department threw outside.

If you can't get a video camera, then use a digital camera and take still photos. If you can't get a digital camera, use a 35mm camera. Use the camera in your cell phone. Heck, use disposable cameras. JUST TAKE THE PHOTOS AND GET YOUR DAMAGES ON FILM!!

NEVER give your film negatives or original videotape to the adjuster. Give copies of the photos and videos, if they ask for them. Keep track of your expenses for photos and videos…you can recover that cost.

Want to know why camera work is so important?

- A photo is worth a thousand words.
- Photos trigger memories, and remind you of building and contents items that were destroyed or damaged.
- Time is of the essence. If you're adjuster can't get to your property for a couple days (or weeks in hurricane losses), and you need to protect your property, you can carefully photograph the areas that you are protecting before you cover them or alter them. That way, you've preserved evidence of the damages.

5. Notify your relatives or closest friends of the loss. Friends and relatives can be extremely helpful to you…but only if YOU control what they do.

- Do NOT take advice from your friends and relatives, unless they have experienced a loss EXACTLY like yours, and were successful in getting every dollar they were owed. If that actually happened, they probably have a copy of this book and followed my advice to the letter.
- Friends and relatives can be great witnesses of the damage. They can help take photos and videos. They can be witnesses when you meet with the adjuster or your contractor. They can make beer runs to the store for you while you're taking care of your claim.

6. Notify the insurance company (See Chapter Thirteen, "Notify the Insurance Company"). It is certainly acceptable to phone the agent or company claim department first, but be aware that many policies require you to report a claim in writing. You'll find a Loss Notice form in the Forms Section of our website that you can download for free. Make sure you know what your policy language says regarding submitting a Notice of Loss. **THIS IS CRUCIAL!!!** If you do not notify your insurance company of your loss in the way the policy says to do it, your claim could be denied.

7. Determine what it's going to take to secure your property and protect it from further loss. <u>This is part of your responsibility in your insurance contract.</u> If necessary, contact a disaster restoration company to board up the building, or tarp the roof, or extract the water, etc. IF YOU DO THE WORK YOURSELF, OR ALLOW OTHERS TO DO FREE WORK FOR YOU, THE INSURANCE COMPANY MAY NOT PAY YOU FOR YOUR TIME.

8. SERIOUSLY CONSIDER HIRING A PUBLIC ADJUSTER (PA) IN THE FIRST 24-48 HOURS (see Chapter Fourteen about Public Adjusters).

9. TIME TO GET ORGANIZED

**Start A File**

You must create a file immediately after your loss. Go to an office supply store and buy one of those cardboard accordion-like expandable folders that can hold lots of paperwork. Even a cardboard box with a lid on it is acceptable for keeping everything inside it. You don't have to be fancy, just keep everything in one place. Your file also must be portable, so that rules out using a filing cabinet.

During the recovery process, place the following in your file:
A. Current copy of your policy. If you don't have a copy handy, call your agent and have him get you a copy <u>immediately.</u>
B. Copies of all written correspondences (don't forget emails) between you and ANYONE regarding your claim.
C. Phone, fax and email address record for everyone involved in the claim.
D. Photos you have taken of the damages...and the repairs. This includes videotapes or still photos of the damages that you took immediately after the loss.
E. A cassette tape of your own recorded statement about how the loss occurred. (See Chapter Twenty Nine, "Recorded Statements")
F. A cassette tape recorder, batteries and spare tapes for recording EVERY conversation that you have with the adjuster, claims examiner, appraiser, engineer, attorney, contractor...ANYONE with whom you

discuss this claim.

G. Receipt envelope. ALL receipts pertaining to this loss should be in that envelope. NEVER give the insurance company your original receipts. They should get copies.

H. Expense log: emergency services, extra expenses, mileage, even extra child care...ANYTHING that you have to pay for that relates to this loss.

I. City, County, and State Building Code requirements in writing.

J. Copy of your state Department of Insurance statutes on Bad Faith Claims, or Unfair Claims Practices. (See the Appendix for a list of all 50 states' insurance departments, and their phone numbers. You can also find this free information at the Forms Button at the website, www.insurance-claim-secrets.com ).

K. Waiver of Lien forms. These forms are also downloadable at the website.

L. Worker's list. A list of everyone who works on your building, who they work for, and what work they're doing. Taking their photo would be a great idea, also.

M. Professional reports, such as an Engineer report, Cause and Origin report, Fire or Police report, etc.

N. Copy of all estimates.

O. Copy of all repair contracts. NO WORK WITHOUT SIGNED CONTRACTS. Also, contractors occasionally find hidden damages that will require supplemental repair costs. YOU are responsible for these costs, even though the insurance company agrees to pay. The insurance company doesn't own your building...you do. GET IT IN WRITING.

P. Copies of any advance payment checks you receive from the insurance company.

Q. If you have a contractor, or ANYONE who works on your damaged property, get a copy of their insurance certificates that show their liability insurance is in effect. No insurance, no work. Period. You CANNOT afford to have a worker get hurt on your premises and file a claim against you for liability or medical expenses. Once you get the insurance certificate, call their insurance company and verify that the coverage is in effect.

## Keep a Journal

Buy a journal book, or just simply use a standard sized legal pad as your claims journal. This means that you should write down EVERYTHING that happens in your claim.

Write down every phone conversation: Date, time, phone number, who you talked to, what was said.

Write down every meeting: Date, time, length of meeting, people in attendance, what was discussed.

Write it down WHEN IT HAPPENS. Don't rely on your memory a few days later. You'll be sorry if you try that.

11. Meet the adjuster. (First, read Chapter Fourteen, "Claims Adjusters") Might be repeating myself, but this is important.

The following procedure is what a professional claims adjuster SHOULD DO at your first meeting:

A.  Introduce himself and give you his business card.
B.  Sit down with you FIRST and explain what he is about to do.
C.  Find out from you if you've ever had a loss before.
D.  READ YOUR POLICY WITH YOU, and answer <u>all</u> of your questions.
E.  Explain in detail the claims process, and the steps he will be taking.
F.  Explain to you, the insured, what your responsibilities are in the claims process.
G.  <u>Then, after all of that</u>…..he should inspect your damage.

If your adjuster does NOT do all of the above, in basically that order…you <u>must</u> realize that you may have a problem right away.

Here's another tip about adjusters. Most adjusters are likeable people, and try their best to get along and be pleasant. Occasionally, you'll find an adjuster who is disagreeable, rude and sharp tongued. If you find that you don't get along with the independent adjuster that has been assigned to your claim, call his supervisor and request that another adjuster be assigned to this claim. Make your request politely but firmly. You do not have to take abuse and poor treatment from an adjuster. If the claims supervisor won't change the adjuster, call the insurance company and ask them to assign the claim to another adjusting company.

If you're dealing with the insurance company's staff adjuster, and getting treated badly, call his supervisor and firmly request another adjuster. If the supervisor doesn't cooperate, go to his supervisor. Keep going up the ladder until you get what you want. If none of this works, call your State Department of Insurance and file a complaint.

Many times you can meet the adjuster at your location on the same day as the loss occurred. That's the ideal situation. Some damages can be mitigated (made less severe) by the speed that cleanup begins. For example, you have a water supply line that bursts in your office, and the red oak wood floor in your conference room gets very wet. If you can get the water up off the floor, and drying equipment in the room quickly, the floor will likely not swell and buckle…and the floor can be saved. If you had to wait 1-2 days for the adjuster to arrive, the floor would likely have to be replaced at much higher cost.

At this first meeting with the adjuster, make requests for advance payments, if necessary (See Chapter Twenty Four, "Advance Payments"). If you've had a major Contents loss, like fire, smoke or water damage, you'll need to replace some of these items quickly. If you have had a loss which leaves you unable to occupy your building temporarily, you'll need money to pay for temporary office space.

Insurance companies will make these types of advance payments to the insured when the advance is requested. They seldom offer an advance.

For    Casualty    Claims    procedures,    read    Chapter    Six, "Comprehensive General Liability".

CHAPTER THIRTEEN

# NOTIFY THE INSURANCE COMPANY

Seems sort of obvious, doesn't it? But, there are <u>different ways</u> to notify the company that you've had a loss. And <u>when</u> you notify the insurance company can make a big difference in how your claim is handled.

The first place to look for information is on your policy. Many policies will have a telephone number listed for reporting a claim. However, I've seen policies that require the policyholder to notify the company in writing. So, make sure that the method of reporting your claim is acceptable to the insurance company. Likely, your agent has his name and telephone number on the policy. If so, call him and report the loss also.

The first thing you should remember is that the agent is a salesperson. It's not his job to handle your claim, but to assist you in buying the coverage that's right for you. Remember that your agent is not a licensed adjuster, he's a licensed agent. He cannot legally help adjust your claim. Agents can be very helpful by making calls on your behalf if you're having problems in your claim. They can be helpful in finding out key names and phone numbers for insurance company personnel that are handling your claim. If the agent has a large number of policyholders with that company, and his clientele represents a large amount of premium to that insurance company, it can be very helpful to have the agent call on your behalf when you're having problems.

After all, it's all about customer service, and keeping the promises in the insurance policy.

Sometimes, the agent or an office secretary/customer service representative will fill out a claim form (called an ACORD form), and submit the claim form to the insurance company on your behalf. In this age of the Internet, frequently the claim form is electronic, and the agent will submit the electronic form by computer.

If the agent notifies the company on your behalf, and uses some type of form, ask the agent to send you a copy of the completed form. Then, you'll be certain that the claim was submitted, and the date the claim was submitted.

Many times, however, the agent will have to refer you to the claims department of the insurance company. Your policy may have a telephone number for the claims department listed on the policy, and instructions how to make a claim.

Your policy requires you to notify the insurance company "in a timely manner" after you've had a claim. What is timely? It varies policy to policy. But each state has statutes of limitation that limit the amount of time after a claim occurrence that a claim can be made. Check with your state's Department of Insurance to determine the statute of limitation where you live…or where the loss occurred. You'll find a list of all of the Insurance Departments of all 50 U.S. states and their phone numbers in the Appendix, and at the website at: **www.insurance-claim-secrets.com** .

For example: you live in Minnesota, and own a retirement home in Florida. The Florida house gets hit by a hurricane. The statutes for Florida would apply.

**WARNING**: If you wait more than a month after your loss to notify the insurance company, they will be instantly suspicious. In those cases, you should expect to receive one of two forms from the insurance company before they begin their investigation of the loss:

1. Non-Waiver Agreement. This basically states that the insurance company is going to do a thorough investigation of the claim, but that their investigation does not commit them to pay the claim. It states that they do not waive any of their rights under the policy, and that the insured does not waive any of his rights by cooperating with the investigation. The insurance company wants the insured to sign this form. However, if the Insured refuses to sign the form, the insurance company will send him a….

2. Reservation of Rights letter. This states basically the same thing as a Non-Waiver Agreement, but the Insured does not have to sign it.

Don't forget to write in your claim journal the date, time, who you spoke with, the phone number you called, and what was said when you reported your claim. That information could be very valuable later if you have problems with your claim.

Most likely, you'll receive a claim number from the company when you report the loss. Write the claim number in your journal!!! Don't expect the insurance company to quickly send you a form that has the claim number on it. Sometimes, it may be many days before the claims department sends you any correspondence, and you will likely need to speak with them before then.

**WARNING:** What about a situation in which someone else is at fault, and you're making a claim against the other person's insurance company? This could happen in an auto accident, or if someone causes damage to your business or business personal property. EVEN IN THIS SITUATION, you must notify your own insurance company that you're involved in a claim.

The reason is that third party claims don't always turn out well for you, the claimant. Sometimes, the other person's insurance company denies liability or denies coverage. Sometimes, the other person's insurance company drags the process out. Sometimes, the other person's insurance company makes a settlement offer far below the fair value of the claim. Months may pass, and you have suffered a financial loss that is not getting paid.

What if you, or one of your employees, is injured in the claim…and the other guy's insurance company won't accept liability?

Those things might occur weeks or months after a loss. In many cases, you can short-cut that process and make a claim against your own insurance policy to repair the damages. Then your insurance company will do something called "Subrogation." That is, they will pay your claim, and then contact the other person's insurance company and demand reimbursement, including your deductible.

So, if you don't report your claim right away, the policy might allow your own insurance company to deny your claim based upon late reporting.

Besides, your policy REQUIRES you to notify the insurance company "promptly" after you have a loss of covered property. That requirement is there no matter who is at fault for the damages.

Don't get caught in this technicality. Don't lose your right to collect what you deserve.

CHAPTER FOURTEEN

# CLAIMS ADJUSTERS

A professional, intelligent, honest adjuster is a pleasure to work with. He treats you with respect and gives his best effort to complete his investigation as quickly as possible. He is patient, knowing that you are not familiar with the claims process. He understands how upset you might be about your claim. He senses that you have already been frightened by the loss itself, and now may be frightened about the claims process.

He explains the process to you before he begins it, and invites you to be an active participant, not a spectator. He sits down with you and reads your policy with you, and explains it as he goes. He makes sure that you have his contact phone numbers, so you can get your questions answered when he's not there. He answers his phone messages promptly.

The following procedure is what a professional claims adjuster SHOULD DO at your first meeting:

1.      Introduce himself and give you his business card.
2.      Sit down with you FIRST and explain what he will do.
3.      Find out from you if you've ever had a loss before.
4.      READ YOUR POLICY WITH YOU, and answer all of your questions.
5.      Explain in detail the claims process, and the steps he will be taking.
6.      Explain to you, the insured, what your responsibilities are in the claims process.
7.      Then, after all of that.....he should inspect your damage.

If your adjuster does NOT do all of the above, in basically that order...you must realize right away that you may have a problem before you start.

Here's another tip about adjusters. Most adjusters are likeable people, and try their best to get along and be pleasant. Occasionally, you'll find an adjuster who is disagreeable, rude and sharp tongued. If you find that you don't get along with the independent adjuster that has been assigned to your claim, call his supervisor and request that another adjuster be assigned to this claim. Make your request politely but firmly. You do not have to take abuse and poor treatment from an adjuster. If the claims supervisor won't change the adjuster, call the insurance company and ask them to assign the claim to another adjusting company.

If you're dealing with the insurance company's staff adjuster, and getting treated badly, call his supervisor and firmly request another adjuster. If the supervisor doesn't cooperate, go to his supervisor. Keep going up the ladder until you get what you want. If none of this works, call your State Department of Insurance and file a complaint.

Many times you can meet the adjuster at your location on the same day as the loss occurred. That's the ideal situation. Some damages can be mitigated (made less severe) by the speed that cleanup begins. For example, you have a water supply line that bursts in your office, and the red oak wood floor in your conference room gets very wet. If you can get the water up off the floor, and drying equipment in the room quickly, the floor will likely not swell and buckle…and the floor can be saved. If you had to wait 1-2 days for the adjuster to arrive, the floor would likely have to be replaced at much higher cost.

At this first meeting with the adjuster, make requests for advance payments, if necessary (See Chapter Twenty Four, "Advance Payments"). If you've had a major Contents loss, like fire, smoke or water damage, you'll need to replace some of these items quickly. If you have had a loss which leaves you unable to occupy your building temporarily, you'll need money to pay for temporary office space.

Insurance companies will make these types of advance payments to the insured when the advance is requested. They seldom offer an advance.

The professional claims adjuster must have empathy for people. I'm not sure if that is a skill that can be taught with a book or a class. Some of the empathy must come from a person's upbringing. Compassion for another human being who is hurting or afraid must come from deep within a person. Even having said this, it is not unusual for a person to have his compassion and empathy stretched thin by the things that happen in life.

For a moment, look at the difficult position that an adjuster is in. He is considered by the law to be in a fiduciary position. That means that he has a duty to perform. His salary or service fee is being paid by the insurance company. So, he must place the financial interests of his client or employer first in the handling of your claim. He must do his best to save money for the company in the payment of your claim. He must do his best to settle your claim for <u>the least amount of money that you will accept.</u>

At the same time, he has a duty to you, the policyholder or claimant, to complete the loss investigation in a timely manner...not stalling or procrastinating. He has the duty to help you file a claim for <u>all of the money that you are entitled to collect.</u>

BUT YOU MUST REMEMBER THIS! It is not the adjuster's <u>responsibility</u> to get you every dollar that you are owed. That's YOUR JOB!!

Let's consider the pressures and influences that work against an adjuster, and how those pressures and influences can affect the claims process for you.

1. Caseload. This is Number One because it's the biggest pressure in an adjuster's workday. Most adjusters I've ever known...including myself...had more cases than they could handle on a day-to-day basis. Then, a big ice storm would come through town or a severe thunderstorm with lightning and hail and tornadoes would blow through the area, and the claims would pile up. There were lots of times that I would look at 12-15 losses per day after a big storm. Normally, I might look at 1-3 losses a day. So, you can see how simple volume of cases can affect the handling of your claim.

The insurance companies and adjusting companies would rather employ overworked adjusters than underworked adjusters. It's cheaper for them in the long run.

2. Work experience and training. Insurance companies and adjusting companies are the same as other big corporations. They know that it costs them far less in salary and benefits to hire a young person than it costs to keep an old seasoned veteran claims adjuster. The old guy has lots of experience and training, and expects to be compensated for it. Consequently, staffing a claims department or adjusting company can be a decision made by managers for economic reasons.

I guess that's a fancier way of saying that sometimes you will get an adjuster who's not trained well enough to handle your claim. Let me give you an example from my own claims adjusting experience.

I had previous experience as a carpenter, then as a builder and general contractor. I know how to build pretty much any kind of building. I've worked with the tools, from shovels to welders to drafting tables to laser levels. I've operated bull dozers, cranes, front end loaders and fork lifts. I know how to read blueprints, how to draw blueprints for a building, and have built two houses with my own hands. In addition to that, I was a property and casualty insurance agent for many years. That's the kind of experience I brought to the claims adjusting business.

Most of the adjusters I've ever known did not have that kind of experience. Many got hired right out of college with their shiny new business degrees, and didn't know one page of an insurance policy from another. The companies they worked for had to spend thousands of dollars and many years sending them through claims adjusting schools. I'm not saying there's anything wrong with that. Getting training is a very good thing. But these young adjusters are not sitting in the bullpen studying their books, waiting for a call to go into the game (forgive the baseball analogy). They are handling claims while they learn. A BIG part of the learning process IS handling claims.

When these young adjusters write estimates, they probably do the best that they can. But many of them really don't know what it takes to repair a house badly damaged by fire or a tornado or a flood. So, their estimates are just that...estimates. It is very difficult for an insured to find a contractor that will agree to do the work in the estimate for the price that the adjuster's estimate shows. That's because it's priced too cheap, and/or they leave out things that will eventually have to be included in a supplemental payment.

Sometimes, adjusters are required to handle claims that are beyond their training and experience, and that adds to the pressure under which they work.

3. Company standards and Department of Insurance statutes. Every insurance company has performance standards that must be met by their adjusters. Sometimes it revolves around the number of files he handles on a monthly basis. Sometimes it is how many files he must close per month. In independent adjusting companies, an adjuster is scrutinized on the amount of billing he submits in a month. That usually determines part of his compensation.

In addition to those pressures, the adjuster must comply with Department of Insurance law regarding Unfair Claims Practices statutes. There are certain things that the adjuster must do to be in compliance, and some of those things have a time limit on them. In some states, penalties for non-compliance can mean jail sentences and big fines.

4. Adjuster experiences.

A. Negative experiences. Adjusters interact with people at a very stressful time in their lives. Some people don't handle that stress very well. Many of those stressed-out people are simply afraid, and take it out on others. When the claims process is not going the way the insured expects it to go, even if his expectation is reasonable, he might say some pretty unkind things to the adjuster. Over a period of years, that can wear on an adjuster and he might get pretty defensive up front.

B. Fraud. Adjusters who have been in the business for a while have seen lots of cases in which the insured/claimant inflates the value of the claim. The adjuster has seen some public adjusters and some personal injury attorneys inflate the value of the claim. A seasoned adjuster develops a sense about whether a claim is valid or not. But, over time, this can lead to an adjuster becoming cynical about everyone who files a claim.

C. Policyholder/claimant ignorance. When I use the word "ignorance," I mean "lack of facts or lack of knowledge." It doesn't mean lazy or stupid. Remember the reason I wrote this book. People do not read their policies. People regularly think that they have coverage for some loss that is not covered in their policy. People do not like to hear that their claim is not covered, and the first person to hear their displeasure is the adjuster.

D. Adjuster attitude. I absolutely love the insurance claims business. I've loved it since the day I got into it. I love helping people and getting paid well to do so. I believe that most people are honest and want to do the right thing.

However, there are lots of people in the claims industry…just like in your business…that don't like their job. Some adjusters have a very cynical, negative attitude about policyholders and claimants. Some adjusters think that everybody is trying to submit fraudulent claims. Some adjusters dislike their job so much that they make everybody around them miserable. I hope, for your sake, that you do not ever meet this kind of adjuster. He can make the claims process a living nightmare.

Adjusters are actually taught in beginners' claims schools to "control" the insureds and claimants. An adjuster can actually get into trouble with his claims manager if he loses control of his insureds and claimants.

What do they consider "losing control?"

Insureds and claimants who don't just accept a settlement…or get an attorney…or get a public adjuster…or are very demanding…are considered out of control.

So, I'm actually trying to train you to be OUT OF CONTROL…THEIR CONTROL. I want YOU to be in control!

Let's talk about the concept of "fairness", and what the word "fair" means in claims. When my children Melissa, Russ and Jarrett complained about something in life not being fair, I always told them that "fair is a place where you take your pig to win a blue ribbon." What I mean is that life is not fair, and they need to get used to it now.

In the claims business, here's a statement that might shock you:

WHAT YOU THINK IS FAIR AND WHAT THE CLAIMS ADJUSTER THINKS IS FAIR IS USUALLY NOT THE SAME THING.

Most states have statutes having to do with so-called "Unfair Claims Practices." (Read Chapter Thirty Two, "Unfair Claims Practices") That usually means that the insurance companies have to deal honestly and promptly with the insured or a claimant. Woe unto an insurance company or a claims adjuster that does not treat the insured or claimant honestly and promptly!

You can also find out more about "Unfair Claims Practices" at your state's Department of Insurance. Look in the Appendix of this book, or go to: www.insurance-claim-secrets.com for more details.

## COMPANY ADJUSTERS, or "STAFF ADJUSTERS"

Many insurance companies have their own claims handling personnel, known as "staff adjusters" or "claims representatives." They are employees of the insurance company, and represent the interests of the insurance company in handling your claim.

Many times, the company adjusters will have the ability to write a settlement check to pay your claim.

Don't ever forget that the staff adjusters work for the insurance company. They'll probably be friendly and professional. But it is their job to settle a claim for as small an amount of money as the insured or claimant will accept.

If you get assigned a staff adjuster by your insurance company, interview him or her and find out how many months or years of experience in claims that person has. <u>Remember</u> that your insurance policy does not have even one word in it that requires you to accept whatever adjuster the company assigns to your case.

If your adjuster has less than two years experience, I'd recommend asking for another adjuster.

If you meet your adjuster and don't have a good feeling of trust, I'd recommend asking for another adjuster.

If you meet your adjuster, and just don't like him or her personally, I'd recommend asking for another adjuster.

If your claim is a property claim, remember that you also can retain a Public Adjuster to assist you. See Chapter Fifteen, "Public Adjusters."

If your claim is a casualty claim (like an auto accident), you should speak with a Personal Injury Attorney, with the understanding that you may need to be represented. (See Chapter Seventeen, "Should I Get a Lawyer?" and Chapter Four, "Business Auto Claims") Also look on my website for more information about legal representation.

## INDEPENDENT ADJUSTERS

The greatest majority of insurance companies will have a claims department that handles its claims, and will use independent adjusting companies to act as their eyes and ears. This simply means that the independent adjuster will investigate the claim and report his findings back to the claims department at the insurance company. Seldom do independent claims adjusters have settlement authority, but can make recommendations to the claims examiner on what course of action might be taken to settle the claim.

Occasionally, the insurance company claims examiner will give the independent adjuster authority to settle a claim, and will authorize the adjuster to negotiate up to a certain dollar limit. If the adjuster can settle the loss for that amount or less, fine. Any demand that goes beyond that dollar limit will likely be reviewed and settled by a claims manager.

I'm going to repeat, almost verbatim, what I said about Staff Adjusters.

If you get assigned an independent adjuster by your insurance company, interview him or her and find out how many months or years of experience in claims that person has. <u>Remember</u> that your insurance policy does not have even one word in it that requires you to accept whatever adjuster the company assigns to your case.

If your adjuster has less than two years experience, I'd recommend asking for another adjuster.

If you meet your adjuster and don't have a good feeling of trust, I'd recommend asking for another adjuster.

If you meet your adjuster, and just don't like him or her personally, I'd recommend asking for another adjuster.

If your claim is a property claim, remember that you also can retain a Public Adjuster to assist you. See Chapter Nine, Public Adjusters.

If your claim is a casualty claim (like an auto accident), you should speak with a Personal Injury Attorney, with the understanding that you may need to be represented. (See Chapter Seventeen, "Should I Get a Lawyer?" and Chapter Four, "Business Auto Claims") Also look on my website for more information about legal representation.

## CHAPTER FIFTEEN

# PUBLIC ADJUSTERS

Public adjusters get their own chapter in this book. I love Public Adjusters.

A public adjuster (PA) is an adjuster that assists an insured who has had a loss in the preparation and presentation of the insurance claim. PAs perform very valuable services to the insured by consulting with the insured on options available in their recovery, filling out forms, helping prepare inventory lists, preparing estimates on structural damages, helping to find you a temporary place to live if you're home is too damaged to live in, assisting in negotiations for settlement...and many more vital functions.

Public Adjusters work only on losses that involve property, such as homes, businesses and public buildings. Those are called "first party property claims."

If you have a loss to your property that was caused by someone else, that is called a "third party property claim." An example is when a vehicle runs into a dwelling, causing damage. In some situations, PAs will accept clients for third party losses. However, PAs cannot directly negotiate a third party claim. They can either advise the client as to the extent and value of the third party loss, or work with an attorney in presenting the claim.

Public Adjusters do not handle Bodily Injury (Casualty) losses, such as happen in an automobile accident. For assistance in those kinds of losses, consult a claims consultant or personal injury attorney.

There's an easy way to understand the function of a Public Adjuster. Compare them to an attorney in a lawsuit, or a Certified Public Accountant or tax preparer when filing your tax forms with the Internal Revenue Service.

Let me ask you some questions:

If someone filed suit against you, would you represent yourself in court? Or, would you just call the plaintiff and say, "You've already got a lawyer. Why don't we just use yours?" Neither choice protects you, does it?

Would you allow the IRS to prepare your tax return for you? If you did, would you expect the IRS to do its best to find every tax deduction for you so that you paid the least tax or got the biggest refund?

Do you file your own tax returns, or do you hire a tax preparation professional to prepare your tax return on your behalf?

Do you hire a tax professional because:

1.  You don't have time to do it yourself?

2.  The IRS has written a tax code that is too complicated for a normal person to understand?

3.  You usually get a larger refund, or smaller tax liability, when you use a professional...because the professional finds more deductions for you?

4.  The fee you pay is usually far less than the additional money you save?

OK then...you've just found comparable reasons to use Public Adjusters.

1.  You need your own experts to help you file your claim.

2.  Policies are written by the insurance companies and are usually complicated and hard to understand. These policies are known as "contracts of adhesion," because they inherently benefit the author of the contract, the insurance companies.

3.  Many people are not willing to take the time to learn about their policies and learn the claims process.

4.  Some people are too busy with work, and family, and life, to handle their own claim...especially in the turmoil immediately after a significantly large claim.

5.  Public Adjusters usually help the policyholder collect hundreds or even thousands more dollars when the policyholder submits a claim. Their fees are a very small percentage of the amount of the settlement.

PAs usually have to be licensed adjusters, and are usually regulated by the Insurance Department of your state. Some states have special licenses for Public Adjusters. Call your state's Insurance

Department office to find out more information about what Public Adjusters can do in your state. You'll find contact information for the Insurance Commissioners for all US states in the Appendix of the book.

Many of the people on the insurance company side take it very personally when a policyholder hires a public adjuster. Many truly believe that the policyholder should just trust the insurance company and adjuster to do the right thing, and not ever question them.

Adjusters and insurance company personnel sometimes play games with their own policyholders when the insured hires a PA. I've heard claims examiners refuse to speak with the insured by phone, telling the insured that, now that they are represented, all conversations have to go through the PA.

However, there's nothing in your policy that states that. Public Adjusters are not attorneys, and the attorney/client relationship is not the same as the relationship between an insured and a Public Adjuster. If your adjuster or insurance company examiner tries to pull that stunt, he's just doing it to delay and cause you problems. Call his supervisor or call the Department of Insurance.

Isn't this amazing? The insurance company writes the policy, makes the rules hard to understand, and then gets mad at you when you hire someone to help you submit a claim. This would be like the Internal Revenue Service getting mad at you because you hired an accountant to help you prepare your tax return.

But it still happens, even though it makes no sense.

The environment is changing, though. Following the hurricane seasons of 2004 and 2005, a newfound respect has grown within the insurance community regarding the value and professionalism of an accredited, licensed Public Adjuster.

Why do you think that the insurance companies and adjusters are not happy when you hire Public Adjusters? There's one big reason. Usually, when a PA is involved, the dollar amount of the claim is higher than a claim without a PA.

When I first got into the claims adjusting field, the "old timers" told me horror stories about public adjuster. They told me how crooked they were, and how they grossly inflated the repair or replacement costs in claims. They told me stories of how PAs were liars and cheats and totally dishonest.

Yet, in my experience dealing with PAs in claims, from homeowner losses to large apartment building fires, to commercial and business losses, I have not met one public adjuster that I didn't like as a person. I have not met a public adjuster who acted in an unprofessional manner. I have not met a public adjuster who wasn't trying his best to make sure that his client...the policyholder who had a loss...got every dollar that was owed to them by the insurance company.

Public adjusters usually represent a client on a contingency basis. That simply means that they help present the claim documents to the insurance company and receive a percentage of the total amount of the insurance proceeds. The average percentage nationwide is 10%. The major incentive that makes the PA work hard is to help the insured get a larger settlement from the insurance company than the insured could have gotten by himself.

The PA is motivated to maximize your claim and expedite the claim adjustment process. It is a balance of making sure that the claim is packaged as completely as possible so you collect every dollar you are entitled to collect without creating unnecessary disputes with the insurance carrier. The PA does not charge for his services until after the claim is paid to you, so they are motivated to get it settled as quickly as possible. Their fee is usually all inclusive, with no additional out-of-pocket expenses. Most established Public adjusting firms can show you how their fee is absorbed in the adjustment process.

You should know that fees are negotiable with PAs. I've seen PA firms agree to substantial discounts from their standard 10% fee on huge commercial losses, and I regularly see 10% contracts on dwelling and small commercial losses. **Caveat emptor...let the buyer beware.** Just be aware that if the PA plunks down a contract in front of you with a blank space where the fee percentage is supposed to be, DON'T SIGN IT!! Negotiate the fee you're willing to pay BEFORE signing the contract. Then let your attorney review it before you sign.

Some state's Department of Insurance regulations cover Public Adjuster fees, and the maximum amounts they can charge for their services. I don't think that's any of the State's business. For the most part, states do not regulate the fees that independent adjusters charge the insurance companies. Why regulate PA fees? I believe that the policy holder and the PA should be able to set whatever fee they can agree upon.

Regardless of my opinion, you need to check with your state's Department of Insurance for this information if you're considering hiring a PA.

You've heard of personal injury attorneys being called "ambulance chasers?" Well, sometimes PAs have to be "fire truck chasers." It is quite normal for PAs to listen in to fire and police scanners and follow the fire trucks out to the location of the fire. It is quite normal for PAs to go door to door in a tornado or hurricane-damaged area and solicit business. There is nothing wrong with this, since it may be the only way to contact victims after a fire or windstorm. That being said, the PA should always be professional, respecting your time and your personal situation.

A professional public adjuster can offer valuable assistance in the preparation of your claim, or even represent you in the presentation of the claim. Hiring a PA early in the claim process can help control the situation and quickly begin the recovery process. The PA can control over-zealous restoration contractors and pushy adjusters. The PA can accelerate and smooth the claim process by walking through the loss with the insurance company's adjuster so they agree on the scope of the loss. This one process can make a huge difference in how quickly your claim is settled, and many times, prevent disputes later on. You may decide that, in your situation, it makes sense to hire a PA in the first 24 hours after your loss.

If you wish to consider hiring a public adjuster, you should treat them just like you treat the adjuster and contractor. Call two or three public adjusters. Meet them, go over the details of your claim, and listen to their proposal of how they are going to represent you.

Get referrals of satisfied customers with phone numbers that you can call and verify. Then, spend the time checking them out. Call the Better Business Bureau about them. Find out if they have a good reputation. Get the insurance certificate and call to confirm coverage.

Once you've checked them out, and if you want to retain a PA, hire the one who checks out best.

Remember what I told you in Chapter Seventeen, "Should I Get a Lawyer?" Don't sign anything without having your attorney review the document FIRST. But, having said that, remember that there may be many things that need immediate attention, like contents removal, emergency board-up, and temporary family accommodations. This means that you should get your PA contract in front of your attorney immediately!

If you've hired a Public Adjuster, you should treat him just the same as the insurance company adjuster. See Chapter Twelve, "Don't Be In A Hurry", with regard to writing down everything you discuss with him. Keep an accurate record of the date and time of all of your conversations, and what was discussed. Record the conversations if possible.

Insist that the PA give you copies of every document he generates on your behalf. Insist on copies of all letters and correspondences between the PA and the adjuster or insurance company.

Your PA will likely have you sign an assignment form, in which you agree to have the PA's name placed on the settlement checks along with yours.

There are only six states in the USA that require the PA to be included as a payee on an insurance company settlement check: Pennsylvania, New York, Virginia, Wyoming, Illinois and Kentucky. That means that if the insurance company doesn't want to be cooperative and place the PA's name on the check, they might not be cooperative unless the law requires them to do so.

In summary, the Public Adjuster will do most of the things for you that are found in this book regarding proper documentation and submission of your claim.

## REMEMBER THIS IMPORTANT POINT!!

You can do all of the things that a Public Adjuster does on your behalf if you'll follow the steps I've written in this book. This will require a lot of work on your part. If you follow my recommendations, you will assuredly collect hundreds or even thousands more dollars in your claim settlement. However, in my opinion, you will collect even more money from your insurance company when you use the services of a Public Adjuster.

For those of you who do not want to expend the effort to handle your own claim from start to finish, and are willing to pay someone to do these tasks for you, then a professional Public Adjuster will perform a tremendous service for you.

Finally, I recommend that you check out the National Association of Public Insurance Adjusters (www.napia.com) for a listing of accredited public adjusting firms in your state. At the website, you'll find helpful links, articles of interest, and information on how individual public adjusters are licensed and accredited through the organization.

# CHAPTER SIXTEEN

# THE SAVANNAH SIREN

Late August in Savannah, Georgia is a steamy delight. The air hangs thick and muggy, and the Spanish moss on the live oak trees barely sways with the slight breezes.

Savannah is a colonial city with a charm all its own. When General Sherman arrived there in December of 1864 on his march to the sea, he found it so beautiful that he did not burn it. Instead, he sent a telegram to Abraham Lincoln, making the city a presidential Christmas gift.

But Savannah is not immune to fires. There have been many over the years. A recent fire has a connection to the John Berendt bestseller, "Midnight In The Garden of Good and Evil."

A fire occurred in the penthouse apartment of a four-story building on the corner of Bull Street and East Oglethorpe Avenue. Our client was the owner of the building, who retained us to handle his claim.

Savannah is a four-hour drive from Atlanta, so I drove down Wednesday afternoon and got room in one of the hotels on East Bay Street, overlooking the Savannah River. At 8:00 Thursday morning, I met the owner at the apartment building. It was already 84 degrees at 8:00 am.

We climbed the long flights of stairs to the penthouse. Our inspection of this 900 square foot, one bedroom apartment found that the fire had started in an extension cord under a bedroom rug (very bad idea). The bedroom had the most fire damage, but every room had substantial damage from both heat and smoke.

The owner only stayed with me for a short while. He identified the tenant as a young single man. The owner told me that the tenant was not at home at the time of the fire, but had come home to find his apartment a total loss. The young man picked through the debris to find some important things, but had abandoned all the rest of his property. The owner's workmen were going to throw all the personal property into a dumpster as soon as I finished.

So, with the exit of the owner, I was left to complete my measurements and take my photos.

Everything started out normally. Measure the room, photograph the damages from various angles. However, I began to notice certain things. In the bathroom, there were curlers, makeup and nail polish. In the bedroom, the closet was filled with long elegant gowns. On a burned vanity table was a styrofoam head with a singed red wig attached.

Then, I went into the living room. On the coffee table were...coffee table books. But these were about Judy Garland and Barbra Streisand. The posters on the walls, although smoky and curled, showcased Broadway musicals, and one poster featuring RuPaul, a female impersonator.

It finally occurred to this somewhat thick mind that I was inspecting the apartment of a transvestite entertainer.

On a marble-topped table was a smoke-smudged post card featuring a photo of eight performers from Club One. One of those eight performers was The Lady Chablis, prominently featured in the Berendt novel about the city. And one of the other performers in the photo was our tenant.

I finished my inspection by 9:30, and drenched in perspiration, I made my way to my car.

I still have the post card.

CHAPTER SEVENTEEN

# SHOULD I GET A LAWYER?

YES!!

YES!!

YES!!

**Remember this important statement:**

**Not knowing your rights is the same as not having them.**

This chapter is likely to be somewhat controversial. I've read and researched a lot to write this book. I've read other authors of how-to claims books, and they're pretty evenly split on this issue. Some think that the average person who gets real well prepared can handle his own claim without an attorney, and sometimes I agree with that. If I didn't, there wouldn't be much use in me writing this book. Many trial lawyers think that nearly everybody needs an attorney in a claims situation. I disagree with that. Many trial lawyers don't take property claims, so they would not be of much help.

Both sides have valid points. Here's what I believe.

<u>I believe we live in a very litigious country</u>. That's another way of saying that people file suit against each other a lot in this country. I believe that you must protect yourself and your business.

<u>I believe that what you don't know can hurt you…it could even change the course of your life.</u> I believe that your lack of knowledge about the claims process could change the destiny of your children's lives and generations into the future. Certainly it won't change your life that much if you just have a small claim. But, if you have a major property loss, or a major liability loss, your life could be very adversely affected. You could be financially ruined and find yourself out of business..

An insurance policy is a legal contract. The insurance company agrees to do certain things and charges you a fee, called a premium. The policyholder (that's YOU) agrees to the terms and conditions of the contract. You usually don't have a choice in the terms and conditions. You either accept them or go find another insurance company. Problem is, most insurance policies are written on the same industry standard forms, so the next insurance company will likely have the same policy language.

I believe that you work too hard to be taken advantage of by an insurance company. The insurance companies have lots of attorneys on their payroll to represent their interests, and will not hesitate to consult them in the settlement process of your claim. Therefore, why should you go through the claims process without benefit of legal counsel? If you send the insurance company a document and ask them to agree to it and sign it, you can be assured that their attorneys are going to look it over before anyone signs the form. Why should it be different for you, the policyholder or claimant?

I believe that every person who files an insurance claim for anything should CONSULT an attorney BEFORE FILING THE CLAIM. This does not mean that you retain the attorney. Customarily, there is no charge for a first visit to an attorney for a consultation, either in person or by phone. But, even if it costs you money to consult an attorney, consider the fee a cost of living your life. But, every person should make informed decisions in their lives, and I do not believe that a person can make a truly informed decision about filing an insurance claim without FIRST consulting an attorney.

To move ahead in a claim without legal advice is to take the chance of relinquishing some of your legal rights. To move ahead in a claim without legal advice is to take the chance of not being paid hundreds or perhaps thousands of dollars that you could be eligible to collect.

"Hey, wait a minute!" I hear one of you say. "I had a car accident and I ran into another vehicle, and I was at fault. My insurance company is going to defend me. It's written in my insurance policy. I don't need a lawyer...the insurance company is furnishing me a lawyer."

Allow me to help you think this through.

Who is hiring the attorney to represent you? The insurance company is!

Who's paying the attorney fees? The insurance company is!

Who is the attorney really representing? The insurance company!!

The insurance company is potentially liable to pay a claim for you up to the policy's liability limits. This could cost them $50,000…$250,000…$500,000…$1 million or more. You'll pay your deductible.

So, whose money are they going to be paying out? THEIRS…NOT YOURS.

They are defending you in your liability claim because IT IS IN THEIR BEST INTEREST TO DEFEND YOU. If they defend you successfully, it will cost THEM less money.

But what if their interests are not your best interests? Who wins? NOT YOU.

I believe that you must consult the right attorney. Don't tell me about your brother-in-law or uncle who practices labor law for some big corporation. Don't tell me about the lawyer who goes to your church…the one who practices real estate law or handles divorce cases. You need an attorney who knows insurance contract law.

I believe that you should NEVER sign ANY KIND OF DOCUMENT OR CONTRACT without having an attorney review it first.

Let me urge you to find an attorney who knows insurance contract law. There are many attorneys who make a fortune representing the insurance companies, but they are not the attorneys who will represent you. Look for a personal injury attorney in your area. Personal injury attorneys usually spend their time negotiating with insurance companies, and filing suit against insurance companies, so they have to be pretty familiar with insurance contact law.

Personal injury attorneys will work on a contingency fee in some cases. That means that they make an agreement with you that they will receive a percentage of your insurance settlement if they're successful in getting a settlement for you. Just remember a couple things:

1. The percentage is ALWAYS negotiable...before you sign a contract.

2. It doesn't usually make sense to hire a personal injury attorney on contingency for a property claim. Attorneys would usually want a much higher percentage of your claim settlement than even a Public Adjuster would. You might just choose to pay him an hourly rate to represent you. That would still be worth it!

3. Talk with two or three attorneys before you choose one.

4. Ask your friends for referrals. They may know a successful personal injury attorney.

5. Even if you decide not to retain an attorney on a contingency basis, have your attorney review EVERY document before you sign it.

6. DO NOT EVER agree to give a recorded statement to the insurance company or adjuster without your attorney present. Do not allow your employees to give a recorded statement without your attorney present. It would be best to do the statement in your attorney's office. But even if it is just a three way phone call, and not done in the attorney's office, you need your attorney to be involved. Read Chapter Twenty Nine.

In closing, a few thoughts about legal representation that you should know:

1. If you actually hire an attorney to represent you, the adjuster must stop communicating with you, and begin working with your attorney. If you have an attorney representing you, and the adjuster calls you, give him your attorney's phone number and address. Then, don't talk to the adjuster or insurance company after that.

2. Most adjusters don't care if an attorney is involved in your claim. In fact, many times they're glad, because they don't have to deal with the insured any more. If you're doing the things I'm recommending in this book, you're going to be exactly the person they don't want to deal with, because you're being so demanding.

3. If the insurance company and the adjuster know you're consulting with your attorney during the claims process, and that you won't sign anything without your attorney's blessing, they will be more careful about what they do. They know you are not a pushover.

4. Sometimes, the insurance companies or adjuster take it as a personal insult that you've retained an attorney. Sometimes, they drag out the process or make it harder for you. Just be aware that this happens sometimes. Also be aware that every state in the USA has an Insurance Department, and there are laws on the book dealing with Unfair Claims Practices. If you want more information about every state's Insurance Department, go to my website at www.insurance-claim-secrets.com and click on the Forms button. The list of all 50 states' Department of Insurance is also in the Appendix of this book.

## SPECIAL MESSAGE FOR RESIDENTS OF USA AND CANADA!

I believe that many people make decisions about protecting their rights based upon their finances. Naturally, for most of us, our pockets are not that deep, and the first question we'll want to ask an attorney is, "How much is this going to cost me?"

The bottom 10% of the population has Legal Aid, or some other government program to provide them legal representation. The top 10 % of the population…the wealthy…keep attorneys on retainer and consult them often. That leaves the middle 80% of the population pretty vulnerable when it comes to legal representation.

For those of you who live in the United States or Canada, there is an excellent solution available to solve the problem of AFFORDABLE legal representation. The solution is a legal services membership, and the company is Pre-Paid Legal Services, Inc. If you'd like to learn more about it, please go to my website at: www.insurance-claim-secrets.com, and click on the button marked "Valuable Links." Scroll down to Prepaid Legal and click on the link. That will show you a short streaming video presentation, and give you an opportunity to become a member of the service if you have an interest.

And yes…if you become a member, I get a commission.

**Not knowing your rights is the same as not having them.**

CHAPTER EIGHTEEN

# DEDUCT THIS!

In most insurance policies, there is a deductible. This is, in essence, your "self insurance" contribution to any loss.

Few policies anymore have a zero deductible, although you can still find them.

The higher your deductible, the lower your premium. The insurance company rewards you for accepting a larger amount of losses.

If you have the financial ability, it's always better to accept a higher deductible. You'll usually save a bunch of premium dollars, since you don't have losses very often.

But you should expect to incur more costs to collect your settlement than just your deductible. In claims, you must be willing to spend some money to collect money from the insurance company.

Insurance claims are getting more and more complicated. Insurance companies are on a mission to increase their profits. That may mean that your insurance company will deny claims, delay claims and defend claims to beef up their bottom line.

The fabled management consulting firm of McKinsey and Company was retained a short time ago by three of the largest Property/Casualty companies in the world. That would be Allstate, Liberty Mutual and State Farm. McKinsey's mission...as always...is to show companies how to earn more profits. Their final report recommended "The Three Ds"...defend claims, deny claims and delay claims.

All three companies have used this strategy aggressively to boost profits for their shareholders. Concurrently, all three have experienced higher than ever complaints of claims handling. Other companies have noticed the higher profits, and will likely follow suit.

I'm including this information in the chapter on deductibles to show you that the claims experience you may look forward to...or have had...or are experiencing right now...is not a mistake, or an isolated incident.

So, what can you do when you have a claim?

First: understand that you cannot just trust the insurance company to take care of your claim for you. They are protecting THEIR money. The moment you file a claim, you become their adversary. If you allow the insurance company to handle your claim for you, you are a fool. They will cut corners and pay the absolute LOWEST amount possible to get you to sign a Full Release and close the claim. You will leave hundreds or even thousands of dollars on the table that you could have collected.

Second: just because you have a deductible on your insurance policy doesn't mean that the deductible amount is all you're going to have to spend. You need to realize that you might have to spend some extra money to collect the money you're entitled to collect.

Like what?

- $50-$200 to have your attorney review ALL the documents the insurance company asks you to sign.

- $50-$200 to get an independent appraisal of your car if it's been damaged.

- $50-$200 to get an independent restoration contractor's estimate of your real estate property if it has been damaged. Many restoration contractors will do an estimate for free, but be prepared to pay for it.

- $50-$200 to have your attorney supervise your recorded statement with the adjuster, or the statement done by your employee.

- $50-$200 for an Independent Medical Examination if you are injured in an accident that was not your fault.

These are just a few of the claims expenses you should EXPECT to pay on your own behalf. Your policy states that it is YOUR RESPONSIBILITY to prove your claim.

But cheer up!! Spending a small amount of money to prove your claim will usually result in you collecting hundreds or even thousands more dollars in your claim settlement.

Let's talk about the deductible you have in your policy right now.

There are a couple ways that deductibles can be handled. For example, if you have a Business Automobile collision or comprehensive loss, you can pay your deductible to the body shop or the glass shop. Then, the insurance company will pay the remaining amount of the claim.

In a Business Personal Property claim, the customary method of settlement by the insurer is to subtract the deductible from the total, and pay the claim. Then, when you begin replacing your property, you have to use your own money equal to the deductible.

Traditionally, in an insurance policy, there is one deductible assessed for each OCCURRENCE. For example, when a tornado hits your building, it damages the building, the outbuildings, the Business Personal Property, and you may have to move somewhere else temporarily. Four separate coverages are affected, but it occurred once. One deductible is assessed.

In some commercial property policies, in which there are multiple locations or multiple buildings on one location, you might find that the policy requires a deductible be assessed for each LOCATION or BUILDING.

After the large number of hurricanes that happened over the last few years in the USA, the insurance companies changed deductibles in locations that were more likely to be struck by a hurricane. In those areas, they usually did one of two things:

1. Added a Wind and Hail Exclusion endorsement to the policy. If you have that endorsement, you likely have NO coverage for wind or hail. Check your policy to see if you have that new endorsement.

2. Changed the deductible to a percentage of the loss. Customary percentages found are 2%, 3%, or 5% of the amount of COVERAGE. For example, if you had a policy with $100,000 coverage on your dwelling, and a 5% wind/hail deductible, your deductible amount is $5,000. Read your policy to determine what your deductible is.

Sometimes a loss is so large that it exceeds the policy limits. For example, your policy insures your building for $500,000.00. The building burns to the ground, and the estimate to rebuild the house is $510,000.00. You have a $1,000 deductible in your policy. In this example, you would not be assessed a deductible. The insurance company figures that your actual loss is greater than your policy limits plus your deductible. So, your deductible is absorbed by the amount of your loss that is greater than the limits.

That's about all I can say about deductibles. The best time to be concerned about your deductible is BEFORE a loss, not AFTER one. Work with your agent to determine what deductible is right for you.

## CHAPTER NINETEEN

# PROPERTY APPRAISALS AND ESTIMATES

In this chapter, we're going to look at how the value of a property claim is determined.

Before we go any further...remember this statement:

THERE IS NOTHING IN YOUR POLICY THAT REQUIRES YOU TO GET MORE THAN ONE ESTIMATE.

Many times, you'll hear an adjuster recommend that you get three estimates. That's just not necessary, and wastes your time and money. That procedure had everything to do with price, but has almost nothing to do with quality and value. Your property is not a commodity…a mere rubber stamp of every other piece of property. It should not be treated like a commodity. Don't let an adjuster get away with this.

Here's another statement to remember:

AN ESTIMATE IS AN APPROXIMATE COST OF REPAIR OR REPLACEMENT OF PROPERTY.  IT IS NOT ETCHED IN STONE. IT IS NOT A CONTRACT TO REPAIR OR REPLACE PROPERTY.

If your loss is an automobile loss, and your vehicle is damaged, it would be best to have your vehicle inspected by the insurance company appraiser and your chosen body shop appraiser at the same time. That way, they can agree on the scope of damages before they start calculating the repair costs.

One of the things I harp on is insisting that your body shop appraiser write an estimate using Original Equipment Manufacturer (OEM) parts instead of aftermarket parts. Don't give in on this point, or you'll be compromising your safety in that vehicle after it's repaired.

In a commercial property loss, in which the building itself is damaged, the claims adjuster will inspect the building for damage. He will photograph the damage and take measurements. He will make notes of all of the damaged items, and note the quality of the building materials. He will note the cause of the damage, if it can be readily determined. All of that information is commonly referred to as the "Scope of Damages."

It would be a good idea to have your chosen restoration contractor meet you and the adjuster at your business location at the time of the inspection. That way, you can all look over the damage, and you, the adjuster and the contractor can agree on the scope.

There should be an agreement between you, the policyholder, the contractor, and the adjuster on the scope of damages. Likely, you won't have a chance to accept the adjuster's scope until he takes the information from his inspection back to the office and enters that information into his estimating software in his computer. Most adjusters will be able to print a copy of the scope and send it to you. <u>You should insist on a written scope of damages from the adjuster.</u>

Don't sign anything without having your attorney review it FIRST.

Adjusters are human and sometimes miss damages. So do contractors. That's why there should be an agreement on the scope of damages…before you ever begin discussing the cost of repairs.

Think about it another way. Let's say you are going to build a new house. Your architect would have to make drawings and specifications of all of the materials that were going to be used to build that house. When it comes time to get bids from contractors, everyone bidding has the same information upon which to base their bid.

It's no different when you're getting bids and estimates in an insurance claim.

Once you have the scope of damages, you can then expect to receive the estimate from your contractor and the adjuster. The best way to handle this is to insist that the contractor and adjuster reach an agreement on the amount of the estimate. Once that's done, the adjuster can report to the insurance company and have them pay the claim.

CONTENTS, or BUSINESS PERSONAL PROPERTY

Get your hands on some catalogs, like Office Depot and Grainger. Get your hands on as many other specialty catalogs as you can find. As you look at the pages of the catalogs, you'll remember the things that you had in your home. You will find hundreds or thousands of dollars in business personal property that you likely would not have remembered owning. Not only will you remember dozens and dozens of items, but you'll have a retail price from a reputable retailer right at your fingertips.

Please don't misunderstand what I'm telling you to do here. I'm NOT telling you to write down items on your inventory list that you did not own. That's fraud, and you can go to jail for fraud. I'm simply showing you a way to remind yourself of things long ago purchased, and possibly stored and forgotten. Don't omit obsolete or unused office products, old stationery, obsolete business machines, unsold inventory, promotional materials, holiday decorations, push pins, thumbtacks, binder clips. That stuff might not have been used in years, but you owned it, and you have a right to collect for it under the terms of your policy. Could add thousands to your claim.

NEW INFORMATION!!

A little while back was handled a commercial fire loss for a century-old mansion outside Atlanta that had been turned into a Bed and Breakfast. The fire was extensive, and the insurance company paid a very large amount on the dwelling alone. Then there was the contents loss which also had pretty high policy limits

This place was gorgeous, impeccably decorated and filled with antiques. I worked with the owners, a young married couple who had both worked in hospitality management for years. Now, they had an inn of their own. It appeared to me that the insurance agent did a poor job of writing adequate coverage on the property, and did not write in an endorsement for Business Income losses.

For months, the couple worked on their Contents list, trying to add everything to the list to reach the policy limits. We were already pretty confident that the loss would exceed the policy limits. However, they were just overwhelmed with this task at the same time they were managing the rebuilding of the B&B.

The insurance company claims examiner called me one Friday afternoon and told me about a company they'd been using recently. This company specialized in writing scope of damages and estimates in Contents claims. This company had some fancy software that worked great in determining the actual Contents loss. The insurance company authorized me to retain this company on behalf of the B&B owners if I deemed it necessary.

The company name is Enservio, and they can be found online at: www.enservio.com

I had a long phone conversation with the VP of Sales and Marketing, and learned about the company. Enservio serves the insurance companies, and that's who pays their fees. They specialize in Contents, whether that is business contents or personal contents.

They get paid exactly like Public Adjusters do, which is as a percentage of their total replacement/repair cost for the report they write. They refuse to work for the Public Adjusters, or represent the policyholder/claimant side of the contract.

What does that tell you?

However, in our conversation, I told the VP that I thought that an ethical Public Adjuster who wrote a very detailed inventory and appraisal performed a valuable service for the Insured. His response was that he would rather have his appraisers use certain "allowances," which translates into lump sums for classes of contents. An example would be to show an allowance for cleaning supplies, rather than actually writing down the cleaning supplies that need replacing. The insured would then have to decide whether the "allowances" were sufficient to indemnify him.

Their claim to fame and success is that they will do a very accurate inspection, and write a very accurate scope and appraisal of the damaged and destroyed personal property.

Because they are a national company, they are likely not interested into handling small losses (less than $25,000). On small losses, their service fee would probably not be high enough for the trouble. I could be wrong, though.

I can see situations in which their services would be helpful...to the insurance companies. Large losses that will have extensive inventories of contents could be completed efficiently, and likely more quickly, by a contents specialty company. Also, in losses in which the Insured hires a Public Adjuster, the insurance company would then have their own expert appraisal for the Contents loss. That would be advantageous for the insurance company if a loss went to trial.

I will not either recommend them for use or warn you away from using them. Their stated goal is to write a very accurate scope and appraisal, and to hold down costs as much as possible. It seems to me that they are, in one sense, becoming the unlicensed Public Adjuster for the insurance industry.

But, isn't the message of this book how to maximize your recovery amounts? Holding down costs is the last thing on my mind.

What that means to you, the consumer, is that they have figured out a way to reduce every Contents loss more than the fee they charge the insurance company. Or else, why would an insurance company hire them to write a contents scope and appraisal? After all, the insurance company already has a staff adjuster or independent adjuster assigned to the claim who is supposed to have these skills.

Another thing that concerns me is that their appraisals must be agreed by the policyholder who had the loss. If they write an appraisal that is substantially less than the policyholder believes he is entitled to collect, what incentive would there be for the policyholder to agree to this appraisal? None that I can see.

I do see that an insurance company, faced with a disagreement between Enservio's appraisal and the Insured's appraisal (or the appraisal of the Insured's Public Adjuster), could take the position that they have a competent appraisal that they accept. Then they could issue a check to the Insured for the undisputed amount of Enservio's appraisal. That would leave the Insured to:

1. Accept the payment.
2. File a complaint with the State Department of Insurance.
3. Invoke the Appraisal Clause. (See Chapter Eight)
4. File suit against the insurance company.

Just remember, you can't hire these people to represent you. The insurance company will have to agree to hire them and pay their fee. My recommendation is to refuse to sign any document in which you agree to accept Enservio's appraisal for your Contents claim as a condition for hiring them on your behalf.

Our Bed and Breakfast owners didn't need the help of the contents specialist company. We carefully documented all of their personal property, and we settled their claim.

CHAPTER TWENTY

# RESTORATION CONTRACTORS

A restoration contractor is very different than a general contractor. Most general contractors who do remodeling or new construction do not have the skills and knowledge that a restoration contractor has.

For one thing, the restoration contractor is very familiar with the insurance claims process, and how insurance companies pay for repairs. The restoration contractors use similar estimating software to that used by the adjusters and insurance companies. A general contractor who submits an estimate in an unacceptable form to the insurance company or adjuster just annoys them, and slows down your claim.

Another reason to find restoration contractor is that they are usually full service contractors. They will be able to do temporary or emergency cleanup and board up. They will own the equipment for drying and water damage remediation. They are familiar with the kinds of damage that fires, wind and water do to commercial building. Finally, they are experts at writing accurate estimates for these specific kinds of damages.

General contractors who do not make their living in insurance restoration do not have this kind of equipment and experience. Period.

Do a search online for restoration contractors in your area. You can also look in your local Yellow Pages under "Disaster Restoration," or "Fire Restoration," or "Water Damage Restoration." Look for logos in the ads that say "DKI," or "RIA" These are professional organizations for restoration contractors. You can also go to the following websites to identify restoration contractors in your area.

DKI - Disaster Kleen-up International. Headquartered in Chicago, IL, is a network of the leading independent property damage restoration contractors across North America. You can ask for a referral at 888-735-0800, and also find them at: www.disasterkleenup.com

RIA - The Restoration Industry Association is the leading trade association for cleaning and restoration professionals worldwide, and the foremost authority, trainer and educator in the industry. You can ask for a referral in your area at 800-272-7012, or the website: www.restorationindustry.org

Call at least two restoration contractors, if possible. Ask them to meet you at your business location to inspect the damage within 24 hours of the loss.

Remember this important point...there is NOTHING in your policy that requires you to get two or three estimates. Meeting two contractors is just a smart way to find one that you like best and want to work with. Interview them about their experience and expertise. Check out their references, and ask them for a list of satisfied customer that you can call by phone. Get a copy of their insurance certificate to be sure they have liability and Workers Compensation coverage. Call the insurance companies to confirm coverage. ONLY AFTER THE CONTRACTOR CHECKS OUT should you hire him.

You might see many restoration contractors drop by after a loss to see if they can help you with temporary repairs, like tarps on roofs, board-up, and contents removal. Don't be annoyed...they are trying to get some new business. Appreciate their effort for what it is. Get written estimates from them BEFORE you sign ANYTHING. They will sometimes tell you that they were sent by the insurance company (maybe true, maybe not), and that it is your responsibility to protect your property from further damage (which is true). They may tell you that they will "direct bill" the insurance company (which they may do).

## WARNING!!

Be very careful on contents removal, sometimes known as "pack out." The more contents they clean, the more money they make. The cost to clean something is usually a fraction of the cost to replace it. However, I have seen restoration contractors charge more to clean an item than it costs to replace it. So, when the restoration contractors are involved, the claim value may be reduced, which benefits the insurance company. That is why many adjusters will bring a restoration contractor with them to the loss location. Remember that many policies pay REPLACEMENT COST, and following major fires, large windstorm and water losses, your damaged possessions could be replaced instead of being cleaned. Every penny that goes for cleaning your contents comes from the contents limit of liability shown on your policy declarations page. So, theoretically, a substantial amount of your insurance money to replace your items could go to the restoration company to only clean the items!! If the restoration contractor cleans a bunch of your property, and you reject it as unusable, there will be less money for replacement of your property.

So, if the adjuster and restoration contractor are all gung-ho to pack-out your property, that's probably a good idea. Getting your property off the loss site will at least prevent it from further damage. But you should be the person that controls which contractor packs out your property. You should also bet the person that controls what gets cleaned and what gets thrown away. This may take you a significant amount of time to sort through, but that time investment will mean a much larger settlement amount.

Under no circumstances allow the adjuster or restoration contractor to make the determination about what business personal property is repairable or replaceable. The adjuster will typically want to clean items and give them back to you. You own the property...it's your call. Fight hard about this issue!

## ANOTHER WARNING!!

Sometimes, adjusters and insurance companies will tell you that you must use their "approved contractor." Unless you can find that requirement written into the terms and conditions of your insurance policy, don't believe it. It's your property. YOU be the person that makes the decision on which contractor or other vendor to use.

The contract for cleaning and restoration of your property will be between you and the contractor...not the contractor and the insurance company. MAKE SURE YOU ARE IN CONTROL!!

CHAPTER TWENTY ONE

# COMMERCIAL WATER CLAIMS

A good rule of thumb about water damage is this phrase: "If the water comes down, it might be covered. If the water comes up, it is probably not covered."

Water damage claims are probably the most common of all insurance claims. Still, you may have a challenge getting your water damage claim paid by the insurance company.

Let's talk first about the biggest water claim, which is a flood. Usually, a flood will cause huge damage to your building, and make it uninhabitable for a time. Everything gets wet, and the water in a flood is usually very contaminated with soil, mud, chemicals and even raw sewage.

The flood loss is also the loss that is most misunderstood. That's because most flood damage is excluded from most insurance policies. Usually, a person must purchase a separate Flood policy, either from an insurance company or through the Federal Government's National Flood Insurance Program.

Sometimes, you have to qualify for flood insurance by living in a designated flood plain. However, that did not matter during the hurricane season of 2004 in Florida, and the Gulf Coast in 2005. There were thousands of businesses that had their buildings damaged by floodwaters that were located nowhere near designated flood plains. The insurance companies denied thousands of claims because the damage was not covered under their normal insurance policies.

The Florida Legislature tried to make the insurance companies pay for flood claims in policies where floods were not covered, but were not successful.

In 2006, a Louisiana court found in favor of Nationwide Insurance Company when they were sued by one of their insureds for denying a claim. The Court found that insurance companies CAN deny claims for wind-driven flood water.

Let's talk about what YOU should do when you have a water loss, no matter what size it is.

## THE MOST IMPORTANT THING TO REMEMBER IS...

## SPEED!

There's a word in the insurance claims business, and that word is "mitigate," or "mitigation." The dictionary defines it as "to moderate in force or intensity." In insurance claims, it simply means to make the damage less, or to stop the damage from getting worse.

The faster you can begin repairs on water damage, the less damage there will be.

Restoration contractors are tremendous assets in water damage claims. Most of us don't know how to clean up water and prevent the water from doing more damage. Most of us don't own the equipment necessary to repair water damage and dry out the wet areas. Restoration contractors do.

You also don't likely know how to clean up to prevent mold growth inside your building. Restoration contractors do. Make sure this gets special attention, because most policies exclude mold damage that occurs from water damage.

Often the restoration contractor is the first one to begin the process of cleanup. Lots of times, the adjuster himself will call in a contractor to do emergency work. They may set up big fans or dehumidifiers. They may pull up all the carpet and the pad. They may even remove some of the baseboards and drywall.

But all that work is vital in drying out your building and mitigating your damage. And, it's normally covered in your policy.

Let's talk about carpet and vinyl flooring for a minute or two.

What if you've bought an expensive carpet for your offices, and the adjuster just thinks it's a builder grade carpet?

Who's going to win? <u>You will, if you prove your case.</u>

There is a way that you can be sure that you receive the exact amount that you should receive to replace your damaged carpet or vinyl. Even if you have replacement cost coverage in your policy, you must know the quality and price of the original to determine the replacement cost.

The most obvious way is to produce the receipt for the carpet you bought. But, what if you don't have the receipt anymore, or it was installed years ago by the builder? What if the receipt got burned in the fire? What if you just bought the building and have no idea about the age, make and model of the carpet?

There is a testing laboratory named ITEL Labs in Jacksonville, Florida. They have become one of the world's most knowledgeable authorities on flooring. They have tens of thousands of samples of carpet and vinyl from the flooring manufacturers. For less than $40, they will send you a packet with a self-addressed return envelope and other bags. You'll cut out a small piece of vinyl or carpet and pad, and send it back to them.

The laboratory will send you a report, telling you the manufacturer, model or design, information about the carpet fiber and the type of backing, and the price of the carpet.

They will do the same for vinyl flooring.

Here's ITEL's contact information:

ITEL Laboratories (Independent Testing Evaluation Laboratories)
6747 Phillips Industrial Blvd, Suite 1
Jacksonville, FL 32256
904-363-0196
Fax 904-363-2379
Website: www.itelinc.com

If your floor covering is worth hundreds or thousands to replace, it will be worth $40 to prove the true cost of your carpet or vinyl flooring.

By the way…the insurance company should pay for the testing of the flooring as a cost of adjusting the claim. However, if they refuse, it's still in your best interest to bear the small cost yourself.

Carpet can be saved in most cases if it gets wet, even soaking wet with clean water. It usually cannot be saved in a muddy flood. The pad underneath the carpet is foam of some sort, and holds water like a sponge. It's very normal for the restoration contractor to pull up the carpet and pad, and dispose of the pad right away.

The backing on carpet will delaminate if it stays wet for too long, and once that happens, the carpet must be thrown out.

Most of the nasty odor associated with wet carpet is found in the pad, not the carpet. Even when you have problems with pet urine, the urine has soaked into the pad, not the carpet. Get rid of the pad, usually that gets rid of the odor.

Sometimes, the carpet can be dried out without removing it from the building. But most commercial carpet is low nap and is usually glued to the subfloor and cannot be easily detached.

Replacing damaged carpet is a hotly contested topic in many, many claims. Most of the time, the claims adjuster simply guesses at the age, quality and price of your carpet. Most of the time, he gets it wrong. Most of the time, his guess on the price is far too low.

Another important thing to do is to get the furniture off the wet carpet as soon as possible. Furniture with legs very often has a metal "shoe" or skid plate at the bottom of the leg. If that metal shoe sits too long on the wet carpet, it could rust, and cause a stain that cannot be removed. Lots of times, the restoration contractor will put the furniture up on wood or plastic blocks. Getting the furniture off the wet carpet also prevents the furniture from absorbing the water and becoming damaged.

Remember the word, "SPEED?"

It's super important if you have wood floors. Wood floors swell and buckle if they get too much water on them for too long a period of time. Many times, wood floors can be saved from damage if the water is removed quickly. Get a restoration contactor to get the water off the floor. Contractors know how to dry out the floor and save it, and that can save thousands in repairs.

Another common source of water damage is water that leaks from a plumbing, heating, air conditioning system or appliance. Many policies will pay for the damage that the water causes, but will not pay to repair the source. For example, if you have a water supply line or drain line that is in or under a concrete slab. The policy will likely pay to access the drain or pipe, but would not pay for the repair of the pipe or drain.

Commercial policies vary as it relates to water that backs up into the building from drains. Most of the time, if you have a clogged drain that backs up within the four walls of the building, the damage is covered. If the sewer outside the four walls backs up into your building, it might not be covered.  READ YOUR POLICY!

Water claims require you to do the same things that any other loss requires of you, which are:

Know what's in your policy.
Keep good documentation and records.
Fight for every dollar of coverage you have.

CHAPTER TWENTY TWO

# THE KILLER FLYING BEER KEG

Or, "Beer kills three motorists, but no one drank a drop."

One of the crazy reasons that I love the claims business is that it provides me with the most bizarre stories. Here is the most bizarre claim I handled in 2005, perhaps the most bizarre ever.

I received this claim from an insurer in London. They insured an engineering company in Florida that did soils testing for a bridge building project. There were two bridges crossing a river, and the State of Florida and Brevard County were rebuilding both bridges. The roadway on either side of the bridge had two lanes northbound and two lanes southbound, separated by a grass median. There was a construction zone about a quarter mile long through the bridge project. Traffic from the southbound lanes was diverted to one lane of the northbound bridge. The posted speed limit in the construction zone was 35 miles per hour. There were all of the barriers, and orange cones, and signage that you'd expect in a construction zone.

Our insured, the engineering company, was a co-defendant in the Wrongful Death lawsuit filed by the families of the three people that died in an accident that happened in the construction zone. The Plaintiffs sued the State, the County, the General Contractor, all of the subcontractors, and the retailer who sold the beer in question. Plaintiffs asserted that the construction zone was designed improperly, and caused the horrific wreck.

Here's what really happened.

Back in 2001, in a four-door '87 Honda Civic was a 15 year old girl, a 16 year old girl, a 17 year old girl and a 25 year old adult male. They had left a beach party near Cocoa Beach and headed to the local beer retailer, where it was their task to buy a full keg of beer and bring it back to the party. On the way from the beach to the store, the 17 year old girl was driving.

They arrived at the store, and the 25 year old male bought the keg. A store employee wheeled the keg out to the car on a handcart, and they placed the keg on its side in the trunk of the Honda Civic. (The store had this on tape from their security camera) They did not secure the keg from rolling around in the trunk. The full keg weighed 140 pounds.

At this point, the three passengers and driver discussed that they needed to get back to the party fast. The 17 year old girl refused to drive any faster on the way back. So, the 16 year old girl volunteered to drive faster on the way back to the beach.

The 16 year old, driving about 60 miles per hour, entered the construction zone driving southbound. Just as she neared the south end of the zone, she lost control of the car. The car went sideways, slid through the grass median, and entered the left active lane of northbound traffic. The Civic was struck right behind the driver's door by a northbound auto. The impact was so strong that it cut the Honda in half. The two people in the rear seats…the 15 year old girl and the 25 year old male, died instantly. The force of the impact spun the severed rear of the Civic, and this centrifugal force caused the trunk to pop open.

The 140-pound keg of beer was sent airborne. It went through the windshield of the next northbound auto, a Saturn four door sedan. The keg landed on the driver, killing him instantly. The driver was a 28 year old male adult, with his mother in the front passenger seat, and a male friend in the right rear passenger seat. The mother was seriously injured, but lived. They were on their way to have dinner at Red Lobster.

No one in either vehicle had drunk a drop of alcohol, yet three died because of a keg of beer.

The 16-year old driver pled guilty to a Vehicular Homicide charge, and spent a little over a year in Juvenile Detention until she turned 18.

The insurance company hired a local attorney to defend the engineering company. We negotiated a settlement with the Plaintiff's attorney. We had a very strong case and were prepared to go to trial to defend our client. However, in order to make the lawsuit go away for our client, we offered the Plaintiff's attorney the amount of money we estimated that it would take for Defense counsel to try the case in court. The Plaintiffs accepted the money, signed a Full Release and dropped our client out of the lawsuit.

I tell this story often because it's so weird, and because it actually happened.

What lessons can be learned from this? How about these?

1. Teenaged drivers do stupid things, and that's the reason they have such high car insurance premiums.

2. Boy drivers are the stupidest, but even girl drivers can be stupid.

3. The company you keep can cost you your life.

4. However sometimes death is so random you cannot plan to prevent it.

5. You should carry very high liability limits on your auto insurance policy. Why? Because plaintiffs usually sue everybody involved in an auto accident. Even though you may not have caused the accident, you could have your life ruined by a lawsuit. Your auto insurance company owes you a defense under your liability coverage, but only up to the policy limits. If you have minimal coverage, just enough to be legal, that's all the insurance company will owe. What would you do if your policy limits were $50,000, and a jury awarded the Plaintiff $300,000? Or a million?

6. Buy a Liability Umbrella policy with limits of at least one million dollars. Two million would be better. The policy is cheap coverage.

# CHAPTER TWENTY THREE

# MOLD CLAIMS

One of the big problems in mitigating a water loss is growth of mold and mildew. Getting the water damage repaired quickly can prevent mold and mildew. Mold and mildew can make a home uninhabitable, causing lots of different health problems, even death.

Take mold and mildew very seriously in your home. Just rubbing some chlorine bleach on it will only bleach out its color, just like when a brunette puts it on her hair.

Special mildewcides must be used to kill the spores and keep them from growing.

Sometimes, even that's not enough to get rid of mold. If the mold has become widespread, it could require major demolition and remodeling. Some molds, like *stachybotrys,* can cause death.

American insurance companies, almost in unison, have very quietly slipped in the Mold Exclusion endorsements into their policies since about 2003. Stunningly, the insurance buyers and consumer groups didn't notice this since the Terrorism Exclusion endorsements were introduced about the same time.

In 2001 and 2002, before mold claims were excluded, mold damage claims were filed with about the same number and severity as fire claims. It's almost as if the insurance companies excluded fire losses, because their exposure was about the same for mold and fire. If they had excluded fire, everyone from Congress on down would have been screaming for their heads on a pike.

Yet few people noticed when the mold exclusion happened.

These claims are basically Water Damage claims, and some type of water damage is still the cause of the loss. The mold grows on the organic material that gets wet, like drywall, wood sheathing and cellulose insulation.

Now, the old water damage claims for property damage can include Bodily Injury and legal defense costs.

There are hundreds of thousands of water damages claims every year. These claims are not going to just go away because the insurance company excluded coverage. The insurers have SHAMEFULLY shifted the cost of repairs to the policyholders and to their lenders.

By the way, if you have a mortgage on your property, it likely has a clause requiring you to provide "all-risk" or "extended peril" property coverage for your dwelling. If your policy now excludes Mold Damage, you are technically in default of your loan agreement. It would be best if you bought Mold Damage coverage BEFORE your lender finally notices the HUGE exposure in their loan portfolio, and requires you to buy the coverage.

Mold has already bankrupted more builders than any other type of casualty loss in history. And so far, Mold Damage Liability coverage for contractors and builders has not been easy to find.

Remember Ed McMahon? He is best known as the sidekick to Johnny Carson of the Tonight Show on NBC. In 2002, McMahon sued his insurance company American Equity Insurance Co., for more than $20 million, asserting that toxic mold sickened him and his wife Pamela, killed their dog Muffy, and made their Beverly Hills house uninhabitable.

A pipe had broken in the six-bedroom home, flooding the family room. Mold spread throughout the house, even spreading into the heating and air conditioning ducts. The cleanup contractors just painted over some of the mold.

The suit was finally settled in 2003 for $7.2 million. This settlement is the highest published recovery in the United States by an individual filing for property damage in a mold lawsuit.

Lots of insurance companies have added a Mold and Microorganism Exclusion to their policies. Check your policy to see if mold is covered or excluded.

If it is excluded, start NOW finding coverage for Mold Damage.

If you had a water damage loss that ended up with mold, you should still be able to collect for the damage that the water did to your property BEFORE the mold grew. Don't just sit idly by and accept a mold claim denial from an insurance company. Go ahead and prove that the water damage happened FIRST, and get your claim paid. Even if you have to file a lawsuit, it could be worth it.

## CHAPTER TWENTY FOUR

# ADVANCE PAYMENTS

Often, when an insured has a loss of significant size, such as a hurricane loss or a fire, an advance payment of a portion of the anticipated settlement is issued by the insurance company.

It is a customary and widely accepted practice for the insurance company to issue an advance payment in this instance. Be aware that there's nothing in the "Loss Conditions" Section of the Commercial Package Policy that deals with advances. It is usually just a courtesy that the insurance company extends to their policy owner.

Here's an example. Joe's Restaurant is hit by lightning, and a fire damages most of the building. Joe's policy has Building limits of $300,000, Contents limits of $150,000, and Business Income coverage. The building can be repaired for $240,000, which is less than the policy limits. However, the adjuster expects that the Contents loss will exceed the policy limits of $150,000, and the BI loss will be $95,000. The adjuster sends in his first report to the insurance company, and tells them to expect the loss to be approximately $485,000 on these three parts of coverage.

The insurance company could easily issue an initial advance payment of $75,000 to $100,000 for Contents, $100,000 to $150,000 for the Building loss, and around $50,000 for the BI loss. But the insurer will not usually volunteer to make an advance payment.

It's best to make your request in writing. Even if it's just a hand-written letter, it's best if it's in writing. Write or type your request, keep a copy for your records, and give the copy to your adjuster. It's also a good idea to send a duplicate copy to the claims department of your insurance company. Send it by overnight courier or Certified Mail. NEVER rely on the adjuster to ask for an advance on your behalf. He might get delayed with other work and it could be days before he asks. DO IT YOURSELF.

Once the insurance company issues you the advance check, go to your bank and open a separate account just for handling claims issues.

Normally, when the insurance company issues advance payments against the BI or Contents losses, the checks will be made payable just to you, because there's no mortgage on your income or contents.

When you ask for an advance against your Building coverage, the insurance company will need to know the name and address of your mortgage company. They will issue the check jointly in your name and the name of the lender. They may send the check to you. If they do, the lender will likely require you to endorse the check and give the check to them. Then, they will set up a system of payments. To find out more about that system of payments, contact the Escrow Department of your Mortgage Company. Every lender is different. Find out what your lender plans to do.

DO NOT DEPOSIT THE ADVANCE CHECK IN YOUR NORMAL CHECKING OR SAVINGS ACCOUNT. Keeping a separate account for insurance claim related expenditures makes it so much easier to keep good records.

ONLY USE THIS MONEY FOR THE CLAIM. Don't take a weekend vacation to Las Vegas with the money, or buy yourself that new motorcycle you've always wanted.

When you receive the other payments for the claim, deposit them in this account. ONLY use this account for the expenses of the claim. When the claim is completed, close the account.

CHAPTER TWENTY FIVE

# THANKS, I DEPRECIATE THAT

OK...I know that's a malapropism, but get over it. I'm trying to make this book somewhat entertaining while teaching you how to collect hundreds or thousands more dollars in insurance proceeds that you're entitled to collect.

I'm an insurance adjuster, not Norm Crosby! (Are you old enough to remember him? He was a stand-up comedian in the 1960s that got his laughs by butchering the English language.)

Nearly every insurance policy that covers some kind of property...homes, contents, automobiles, commercial businesses, trucks and their cargo, ships and their cargo...deals with the valuation of the insured property.

Most property coverage starts out by insuring property for its ACTUAL CASH VALUE, or ACV. Permit me a few moments to explain what ACV is.

We'll start with the other concept in property valuation, and that is REPLACEMENT COST VALUATION, or RCV. That simply means the cost to replace any item that is insured. For example, you have a 2007 Toyota Celica and you paid $20,000 for it. If the car got in an accident and the damage was a total loss, it might cost you $22,000 to buy a 2009 Toyota Celica exactly like the damaged car. So, $22,000 would be your Replacement Cost.

It works just like that on any item of property. It also works kind of in reverse on items like electronics. If you bought a laptop for $1,500 in 2006, chances are that the same laptop in 2009 costs $999.00 or less. But, that's still the RCV.

Some insurance brainiacs argue that RCV contradicts the principle of indemnity, which is restoring the insured to his pre-loss condition. But the insurance companies designed RC coverage to answer a market need, and they charge an extra premium for RC coverage. So all parties benefit.

Remember that in a policy with Replacement Cost coverage, the highest recovery amount is the policy limit. But it you had a policy with "guaranteed replacement value," the policy might pay an amount that exceeds the policy limit.

Let's try to understand the word "Depreciation" as it relates to RCV and ACV in insurance.

Every article of property has a useful life. For example, your washing machine may have a useful life of ten years. If the washing machine was worth 100% of its value when you bought it, and it has a useful life of ten years, then it loses 10% of its value each year. By the tenth year, it has an ACV of $0. That doesn't mean that you should throw it away. That doesn't mean it doesn't still work great. We're only talking about ACV.

Depreciation is affected by more than just age. Wear and tear are big important factors in determining depreciation. If that washing machine has a ten year useful life, that's under perfect conditions. But if it get used hard, and not maintained well, that will shorten its useful life.

Think about the useful life of what goes into that washer...your clothes. Clothing has a short useful life. That nice pair of slacks you bought might only have a useful life of 2 or 3 years. If it were 2 years, then the slacks would depreciate 50% per year. At 3 years, the slacks would depreciate 33% per year. Children's clothes can get worn out in 3 months.

In business, the tax laws have depreciation tables for all kinds of property. Sometimes, depreciation is allowed for a short period of time, and some depreciation is spread out over years. Many times, insurance companies will want to use tax depreciation as the standard for adjusting a loss. But tax depreciation is way different than actual depreciation. Don't just accept the depreciation assessed by your claims adjuster. It could cost you thousands of dollars.

The insurance company or adjuster will determine the Replacement Cost Value of an item of property...the RCV. Then, he will factor in the useful life and the condition of the property at the time of the loss...that's the depreciation. He'll subtract the depreciation from the RCV, and the sum remaining is the ACV...the Actual Cash Value.

OK...do you understand the concept of Depreciation, RCV and ACV now?

Let me give you the best two examples of ACV I know.

1. Go to a garage sale, and buy something used. What you paid for that item that day is its truest ACV.
2. Go to the wonderful auction site Ebay. Look at the prices sellers are getting for selling something used at auction. Those prices for that item that day are its truest ACV.

Let me explain to you why this is important in EVERY PROPERTY INSURANCE CLAIM.

You are going to get paid based upon the valuation of your property by an adjuster and the insurance company who insures your property.

Even in a liability claim, the same thing happens with adjusters and insurers. If your vehicle is struck by another vehicle, and the accident is his fault, and your car is a total loss…the other guy's insurance company is going to try to depreciate your car in the settlement.

But, it's not just the "other guy's" insurance that's going to try to take advantage of you.

Your own insurance company is going to try to "lowball" you, or get you to accept the lowest possible amount of money in settlement.

Here are the most important two questions that exist concerning depreciation:

ARE YOU READY??

HERE THEY COME!!!

1. Who determines the correct amount of depreciation?
2. What method is used in determining depreciation?

Answer to Question 1:

The insurance company will determine the amount of depreciation that is subtracted from the replacement cost of your property UNLESS YOU CHALLENGE THEIR FIGURES.

Answer to Question 2:

A. Insurance companies and insurance adjusters use published depreciation tables to determine the useful life and depreciation of a vast assortment of property. I have posted depreciation tables in the Forms Section on my website that you can print off for yourself. I've also listed links below that you can click on to see other depreciation tables.

B. Most adjusters and claims departments these days have sophisticated estimating software that has the depreciation tables built right into it. So, when the adjuster writes his estimate, he will enter certain data, like the age and condition of the property, and the estimating program automatically depreciates the property.

C. Lots of times, an adjuster will use his experience and just take a wild guess. This is sometimes known as "Gut Depreciation". It's a wild guess based on past experience in calculating claims. You might have heard this sort of guessing called a WAG (wild-a** guess) or a SWAG (scientific wild-a** guess) or an EWAG (educated wild a** guess). You would be very surprised how often a WAG, EWAG or SWAG is used in an insurance adjuster's life. You'd also likely be surprised how often adjusters' WAGs are accurate.

But now, let's consider how this depreciation, RCV, and ACV stuff affects YOU in your claims.

The CP0010 Building and Personal Property Coverage Form pays ACV on covered losses. Here are is the actual policy language:

E. Loss Conditions, 7. Valuation

"We will determine the value of Covered Property in the event of loss or damage as follows:

a. At actual cash value as of the time of loss or damage..."

Most insurance companies have an endorsement that you can buy that provides replacement cost valuation on your Business Personal Property. The premium is only a few dollars more, and you should NEVER be without this endorsement on your policy. If you find that you do not have this Replacement Cost (RC) coverage on your BPP, DO NOT LET ANOTHER 24 HOURS PASS BEFORE YOU ADD IT TO YOUR POLICY.

So, if you have Commercial Property loss, and you don't have the RC endorsement, the adjuster is going to depreciate ALL of your BPP.

The policies usually specify LIKE kind and quality for replacement. But commercial property policies do not say anywhere that replacement must be with identical kind and quality.

Insurers often resist paying RCV on contents that are not replaced item-by-item. However, the insurance company could be persuaded to pay if you show them this quote from FC&S, the industry authority on insurance matters:

"An insured who has coverage for replacement is not required to replace each and every damaged item in order to receive replacement cost.... The insured is not required to replace every item that was involved in the original statement. Nor is the insured required to use any part of the ACV recovery on any one item of insured property to pay for all or part of the replacement cost of another item of insured property." FC&S Bulletins, Q&A 811 (January 1991).

The insured does not have to spend more than the ACV of the loss amount to qualify for RCV payment. The depreciation holdback should be paid to the insured as the items are replaced.

Further, the insured does not have to replace a building on the same property to qualify for replacement cost. Purchasing another building in another location can qualify for RCV, even if the purchase is in another town or even another state. For example, an insured has a factory in Minnesota and another in Florida. The Minnesota plant is destroyed. The insured can buy a building next to the Florida plant and move operations there. That will qualify for replacement cost recovery, but will be based upon replacement cost in Minnesota.

### The Holdback Trap And How To Beat It

If you have a policy that has the Replacement Cost Valuation endorsement for BPP, the adjuster and insurance company are going to use depreciation to create something called a "holdback of recoverable depreciation." The insurers state that they only owe the ACV until the insured actually replaces the damaged property.

So, even if you have the RC Endorsement on your policy, the insurance company will hold back the recoverable depreciation until you replace your damaged property. If the adjuster doesn't calculate depreciation correctly, the insurance company could withhold hundreds or thousands of dollars from you that you need to replace your damaged property.

That's the trap. The insured only gets ACV up front from the insurance company, and then has to finance a portion of the replacement themselves and wait for a reimbursement. And, the insurer gets a few extra weeks or months before they have to pay policy benefits. Some businesses find themselves cash starved after a loss, and funding the replacement purchases would be nearly impossible. A "walk-away" can help in this situation.

Ever hear of a "Walk-Away" settlement? This happens when the insurance company and the policyholder agree to a settlement amount that is somewhere between ACV and RCV. By accepting the walk away, the insured agrees not to present a supplemental claim for the RC holdback amounts at a later date. This can be an acceptable outcome for both sides: the insurer pays less than replacement cost, and the policyholder gets more money up front. This is especially advantageous for an insured that had obsolete inventory that he was not going to replace. It could also be a winner for a business owner who decided not to reopen his business after the fire. This method of settlement also saves a lot of time for both the insured and the insurer.

Remember the reason I wrote this book? To show you how to collect hundreds or thousands of dollars MORE in settlement that you are entitled to collect?

Well, you are entitled to a VERY ACCURATE calculation of your Building and Business Personal Property loss.

Here are the things that YOU MUST DO.

1. Go to the website at: http://www.insurance-claim-secrets.com Click on the Forms button. Find the Contents Inventory form. Print a form and make as many copies as you need. This is what you're going to submit to the adjuster or insurance company to document your BPP loss.

2. List everything that has been damaged…down to the last thumbtack, extra box of pens and paper clips. Hey…you paid for this stuff. If it got damaged in a covered loss, the insurance company is bound by their contract with you to make you whole again. There is NOTHING that you own that is too small or insignificant to be listed on your Contents Inventory form.

3. List the age of every item to the best of your ability. In a fire or tornado or hurricane loss, there could be hundreds of items that you don't have receipts for. But that doesn't mean they didn't exist. List them.

**Here's a terrific tip.** Pictures are worth a thousand words. Get copies of catalogs you use, like Office Depot or Grainger, and other specialty catalogs if necessary. Then take the inventory list and start thumbing through the pages. You'll be amazed at the things you'll remember owning that should be on your inventory list. Not only will the catalogs stimulate your memory, but give you the latest price of that item right in front of you. Sure, some of your stuff may be of higher quality than what you find in the catalogs, but if you're in a hot negotiation with the insurance company over the value of your contents, you're assured that you should get at LEAST the value found in the catalog.

4. Produce as many receipts and invoices as you possibly can to prove that you owned your contents. Receipts will also prove the age of the items automatically.

5. Remember when I told you to photograph or take video footage of every room, every closet, every drawer in your desks, and put that tape in your safe deposit box or some other secure offsite storage? Now is the time to get that tape and look it over. The insurance company may want a copy of the tape. Give them a copy if they ask, but only if they ask. Don't EVER give them your original tape.

6. Require the adjuster or the insurance company to provide you with a copy or copies of the exact depreciation tables that they used to determine the depreciation on every item of your Inventory list. Once you have the tables, you can compare each item to the tables to make sure that you are paid exactly what each item is worth.

7. What if you find that your adjuster or insurance company has used the WAG/SWAG method? DO NOT ACCEPT IT. There are depreciation tables for nearly everything. Insist on receiving the depreciation tables that the adjuster or insurance company used on your claim.

You need to have access to depreciation tables that are industry accepted tables. So, here's another resource for anyone with a computer and the ability to go to a website.

Go to: http://www.claimspages.com

At the top of the homepage is a blue horizontal bar that has words in it. Move your cursor to the right until it is over the word "Tools." Click on it. Move your cursor down to "Depreciation Calculator." Click on it.

Now, a page will open that allows you to find a depreciation schedule either by keyword search, or on another drop down menu that lists every type of property from different categories.

This is a SUPER tool! This tool will get you hundreds…possibly thousands of dollars more in your Contents claim, because the depreciation will be accurately calculated.

Once you prove that you've replaced the damaged property, the insurance company will release the holdback amount to you.

You see, it's simple…but not easy!

## The 180-day Replacement Clause

Many people, including adjusters, misconstrue or misunderstand the policy terminology on replacement cost coverage. They say that the insured has 180 days from the date of loss to make repairs and submit their documentation to receive the replacement cost recovery. But this is not true! Most policies state that the insured has to notify the insurer within 180 days of his INTENT to use the replacement cost clause. That's what it states in the CP0010 Form.

The best way to handle this loss condition is for the insured to notify the insurer of their intent to recover depreciation holdback amounts in writing, Certified Mail, within the first few days after the loss. That way, you never miss a deadline.

These kinds of negotiations and claims processes can be treacherous, nerve-wracking, time-consuming and just downright difficult. You have a business to run. It's even more crucial after a loss to concentrate on the business to assure its survival. That is why retaining a Public Adjuster is so beneficial to a business owner. The PA can do all the calculations and negotiations on your behalf and they customarily get you a higher recovery amount.

So, I strongly recommend retaining a Public Adjuster for your loss.

CHAPTER TWENTY SIX

# CO-INSURANCE CLAUSE

There is one portion of a commercial property insurance policy that is extra confusing to most policyholders. That is the principle and practice of Co-insurance.

<u>If you don't understand this part of the insurance contract, it can cost you thousands of dollars at claim time.</u>

In a Building and Personal Property Coverage Form like CP0010, there is a section entitled "Additional Conditions." Section F. 1. is where you'll find "Co-insurance."

Go find your policy and turn to the Conditions section, and read the part labeled "Co-insurance."  I thought about putting a copy of the section in this chapter to make it easy for you. But the reason I'm writing this book is to shake you up and get you more involved in your own claim. You're going to get paid hundreds or thousands of dollars more because of the stuff in this book, and you're not going to give me any of it. So, get busy and read your policy.

Let me at least translate the legalese:  The insurance company requires you to carry policy limits on the Covered Property equal to no less than the percentage shown in the Policy Declarations.  If you do not carry that percentage of the full replacement cost, the insurance company will penalize you when you have a claim.

Simple.  But dangerous for your cash flow.

If you have a building that has a replacement cost of $1 million, and your policy limit for the Dwelling is $1 million...no penalty! You're insured 100% to value. You really should be insured 100% to value all the time.

Please remember that being insured to value does NOT mean that you insure your building and other property for its market value or sale price. Insure the Covered Property for the amount of money it will take to rebuild or replace the Covered Property completely. Don't include the cost of the land your building sits on. Insurance companies don't insure dirt.

Insure your property for anything less than the percentage shown in your policy and there could be a coinsurance penalty.

There's a simple formula to figure co-insurance:

What you DID buy divided by what you SHOULD have bought.

$$\frac{\text{DID}}{\text{SHOULD}} \text{ x loss minus deductible = claim amount}$$

Here's a quick example:

| | |
|---|---|
| The value of the property | $250,000 |
| Coinsurance percentage | 80% |
| The limit of insurance is | $100,000 |
| The deductible amount is | $250 |
| The amount of the loss is | $40,000 |

Step 1: $250,000 x 80% = $200,000 (the minimum amount of insurance to meet your coinsurance requirement)

Step 2: $100,000 (what you did) divided by $200,000 (should have done) = .50, or 50%

Step 3: $40,000 x 50% = $20,000

Step 4: $20,000 - $250 = $19,750

The remaining loss balance of $20,250 is not covered.

You see? It really is quite simple to figure out.

Sometimes, there is a coinsurance requirement on the Contents portion of the coverage, too. The same rule applies, and the same method of figuring out if there's a penalty applies.

The BIG problem is that most people don't figure out that there is a coinsurance problem until AFTER they have a loss of some kind.

There are a few obvious reasons that property is under-insured:

1. When you filled out your insurance application, you used a figure that is too low for replacement cost of your property. This could come from:

A. Ignorance...meaning you don't really know how much it would actually cost to replace your property.

B. Simply using the same policy limits on your new policy as you had on your old policy.

C. Being too cheap, and buying a policy with lower limits to save premium dollars.

2. Your agent doesn't know what it would cost to replace your property when he submits the application.

3. The agent was bidding low price to get your business, and made some cuts to get the premium down.

### About the only thing that you can do to minimize a coinsurance penalty is to challenge it.

If your adjuster tells you that you will have a coinsurance penalty assessed against your claim, make him provide his calculations of the coinsurance penalty.

The first thing that the adjuster has to do to calculate coinsurance is to calculate the valuation of your property. EVERYTHING ELSE he does is based on that calculation. If it's too high, your coinsurance penalty will be too high.

He will calculate either the Replacement Cost Valuation (RCV) or he will calculate the Actual Cash Valuation (ACV). The policy will tell him which valuation to use. He doesn't get to choose on his own. Most Homeowners policies are RCV on the dwelling. Most commercial property is ACV, although an endorsement for RCV is available for a small extra premium.

To calculate the property valuation, the adjuster can use:

1. A Wild A** Guess (often done)

2. His estimating software. Some estimating software has valuation built in, so all he has to do is enter data about the age and condition, the size of the building, the features, etc., and that software will do the work for him.

3. Marshall and Swift (M&S). The absolute standard in the insurance industry for building valuation is a company called Marshall and Swift. All adjusters know about M&S, even if they don't know how to use their database. (If your adjuster doesn't know about M&S, or how to use it, get another adjuster FAST.) Even if the adjuster uses M&S, you need to review the data he entered to obtain the valuation. If he entered wrong data, the valuation will be wrong, too. For example, if he used the area of your building at 20,000 square feet, and your house is only 16,000 square feet, the entire valuation will be wrong.

There are a bunch of variables that are entered into a valuation software program that have a DIRECT bearing on your valuation.

Things like the following:

Age
Condition
Size
Number of rooms
Maintenance
Finishes and extras
Basement or slab foundation

## SUPER HOT TIP!!!

YOU can now use the Marshall and Swift valuation program, just like an adjuster. They have built a website where any person can go and calculate their own property valuation. They charge about $8-$15 for each valuation. There is a tutorial on the home page of the website, which will tell you exactly how to use the program. It's super easy and very accurate.

Go to: http://www.swiftestimator.com

\*\*\*\*\*\*\*\*\*\*\*\*

Remember, require your adjuster to furnish a copy of his valuation calculations for your property. Compare it with the Marshall and Swift valuation to make sure it's accurate. If you don't have the ability to get your own valuation, take the adjuster's valuation and show it to a real estate broker. Not just an agent, but a broker. The broker will likely be able to look at your property and the valuation, and tell you if it's accurate.

If you have calculated a lower valuation than the adjuster, insist that he use your valuation for his coinsurance calculations.

If you're reading this book BEFORE you have a claim, call your agent and make sure that you are insured to value.

If you're reading this book AFTER you have a claim, call your agent and ask him why you're NOT insured to value. If your agent messed up, and you can prove it, you could have grounds to make a claim against your agent's Errors and Omissions Liability coverage.

If you're reading this book to figure out how to collect every dollar you're entitled to collect, then...

**FIGHT FOR EVERY PERCENTAGE POINT!!** Every percentage point of a coinsurance penalty is worth hundreds or thousands of dollars. Don't allow yourself to be cheated out of all of the money you are entitled to collect.

CHAPTER TWENTY SEVEN

# NEW ORLEANS SEWERS BACKED UP?

Hurricane Katrina was responsible for one of the largest and most interesting claims I've handled. It was also one of my biggest successes. I'm going to have to be somewhat vague in this chapter, since specifics would give away the identity of the policyholder. The insurance company has requested that I keep that to myself.

Katrina hit New Orleans on August 29, 2005. We got this assignment about a week later. Our insured had two multi-floor buildings in the west end of the city. They had been flooded to a high water mark of about five feet on the first floor. There was some slight roof damage on the main building, but a big chunk of the adjacent building's roof was torn off by wind and rain did its work on the inside of the building.

The insurance company sent me a copy of the policy. We knew right way that there would be a problem, since there was a sub-limit of Flood coverage of only $250,000. Kind of crazy for a policyholder in a city below sea level, but that wasn't my call.

We contacted the owners and began to try to gain access to the building. But Mayor Ray Nagin invoked a curfew on the city that kept most everyone out. He lifted the curfew at midnight, September 28th. That day, I got in my car and headed for New Orleans from Atlanta. The closest hotel room I could find was about an hour south of Montgomery, Alabama, still hundreds of miles from the Big Easy.

I arrived at the first checkpoint at about 9:30 on Thursday the 29th. A National Guard soldier, carrying an M-16 with a fixed bayonet, checked my papers and asked me if I was armed. I showed him my twin Glock .45 pistols and he waved me through.

Driving into New Orleans from the northeast was a surreal experience. There were almost no people in the city. Only occasionally would I see a police cruiser, an Army vehicle or a pickup truck from a restoration contractor. It was just mile after mile of empty houses and buildings. There were thousands of cars and trucks strewn around the streets and neighborhoods. It looked like a child had taken a grocery bag full of Matchbox™ cars and poured them out on a miniature cityscape.

I arrived at the insured's buildings and met the owner and his contractor. The water had receded and it was somewhat safe to enter the building. So we grabbed our flashlights, donned our boots and headed inside. In the dark rooms, the flashlight beams were filled with mold spores. (I got a lung infection two weeks later)

When we finished our inspection, we agreed that the contractor would submit an estimate to be compared with the one I would write. I also reminded them again that their policy limit for Flood was only $250,000. Then I went back to Atlanta. Shortly thereafter, I resigned from that adjusting company and took a job with a larger company. I forgot about the loss.

Over time, the claim grew. Eventually, the policyholder hired a lawyer who proffered a very interesting theory of causation. He knew that millions of dollars of flood damage was not going to be covered under the policy. So, he stated that the city sewers had backed up in New Orleans, and that backup of sewers and drains was the cause of the flood. Coincidentally, damage due to sewer backup was covered in the insured's policy. He also make claim for Loss of Income, even though the policy clearly stated that there was no coverage.

But sewer backup? The levees had failed, as the whole world witnessed. Nearest the levees the water covered entire houses. At the policyholder's end of town, the flood water was only 5 feet deep. In addition, when sewers back up, the water pressure lifts off manhole covers in the streets. There was no evidence whatsoever that manhole covers had ever moved an inch.

The insured and his attorney finally submitted a claim just over $16 million. The insurance company paid them the sub-limit of $250,000, and then the fighting began.

The insured filed suit against the insurance company. The insurance company filed a countersuit.

In 2008, the attorney representing the insurance company contacted me and retained me as a claims consultant. My task was to carefully review the insured's claim and make recommendations on what could be paid and what should be denied. Because I was the adjuster who had begun the claim in 2005, the attorney determined that I would be the most valuable person to evaluate the claim.

The policyholder simply wouldn't submit proof of their claim. Over and over, we requested that they provide proof of the claim and they just ignored the requests. What kind of proof? Oh, simple things like telling us what rooms matched the repair invoices, and what caused the damages in those rooms. After that, we had a day of depositions, and I was interviewed under oath by both attorneys.

I submitted my huge final report. Most of my report went line by line for hundreds of pages and requested proof of the claim. It was impossible for the insurance company to determine what was covered without the documentation provided by the policyholder.

Finally, in late fall 2008, the insurance company, the insured and a bunch of attorneys appeared in a courtroom in New Orleans. The judge reviewed my extensive report and the attorneys' pleadings. Then they went to work.

The insurance company and the policyholder settled the claim at $3 million, which included all flood and wind damages. The court denied the Loss of Income claim.

The insurance company and the attorney were pretty happy with me, since they had just saved over $13 million dollars. They paid my fee pretty quickly.

I don't think that the policyholder will get to keep the money, though. They had received millions from FEMA as well as the State of Louisiana's "The Road Home" program. Those programs will be looking to get their money back.

Sewer backup, indeed!

CHAPTER TWENTY EIGHT

# HURRICANE CLAIMS

Thirteen major hurricanes have hit the coastal US since summer of 2004. They are named:

Charlie - landfall in Florida, Category 4
Gaston - landfall in South Carolina, Category 1
Frances - landfall in Florida and Alabama, Category 3
Ivan - landfall in Alabama, Category 3
Jeanne - landfall in Florida, Category 3
Dennis - landfall in Florida, Category 4
Katrina - landfall in FL, AL, MS, and LA,   Category 4
Rita - landfall in Louisiana and Texas, Category 4
Wilma - landfall in Florida, Category 4
Dolly, Fay, Gustav, and Ike, Gulf Coast in 2008

These thirteen hurricanes caused damages far in excess of $250 billion dollars.

Climatologists at the National Climactic Data Center (www.ncdc.noaa.gov) and the Department of Atmospheric Science at Colorado State University say that they expect the next few years to be equally severe as 2004 and 2005.

Filing a claim after a hurricane has its own little quirks, but the process is pretty much the same as any other claim filing. If you follow the directions in this book, you'll probably come out far better than your neighbors who haven't read this book. But, don't be an un-neighborly neighbor. Tell them the website address so they can get one of their own. Or, tell them to go to their favorite bookstore and pick up a copy. Or, buy them one and be really nice.

When a hurricane strikes where you live, here is what you should do to protect your property and protect your insurance claim.

AFTER THE STORM

1. When you can safely get to your property, inspect the property and find out what needs to be done.
2. Take a camera, lots of film (or disposable cameras) and a pad of paper. Photograph ALL DAMAGE, INTERIOR AND EXTERIOR. TAKE PHOTOS OF CONTENTS DAMAGE. There might be hidden damage...don't worry about that. Just get photos of the damage in plain sight. Don't wait for the adjuster to do this. He might be days or weeks from inspecting your property. <u>Your insurance policy requires you to mitigate your damage.</u>
3. Describe in writing on your pad of paper all of the damage you can see.

4. ONLY THEN should you think about mitigating your damage. Remember, the word "mitigate" is an insurance term that means protecting the property from further damage. This can be placing tarps over damaged roofing, or pumping water out of your building or other temporary repairs. The costs for temporary repairs to protect your property are covered in your policy.

5. GET YOUR POLICY AND READ IT. Notify your insurance company that you have a claim. See Chapter Thirteen, "Notify Your Insurance Company."

6. DON'T THROW ANYTHING AWAY QUITE YET. If you're making a pile of debris, make sure you photograph and write down everything that goes into the pile.

7. CALL A PUBLIC ADJUSTING COMPANY AND HAVE THEM EVALUATE YOUR LOSS. See Chapter Fifteen.

8. CALL AN ATTORNEY WHO KNOWS INSURANCE CLAIMS LAW. See Chapter Seventeen, "Should I Get a Lawyer?"

Let me give you a few basic guidelines about claims after a hurricane.

You should realize right now that thousands of other people have damaged property, and insurance company response is going to take some time.

Having said that, please remember that the old saying "A squeaky wheel gets the grease" is even more true in a catastrophe situation. Claims adjusters and company claims examiners are human, and they don't like to be annoyed any more than you do. If you are constantly, relentlessly, politely demanding, they will place your claim at the top of their list. They will want to get rid of you, and the way to do that is to get your claim paid.

I promise you that most of the people filing a claim will patiently wait like sheep waiting to be shorn. <u>If you will do what this book says, you'll get more money and get it sooner.</u>

Also, if you retain a Public Adjusting company, they will expedite your claim, and characteristically help you collect far more money.

You should be aware right now that insurance companies send adjusters and temporary adjusters called "Storm Troopers" to your area to help with the overflow of claims.

"Storm Troopers" are people who are trying to do a good job as adjusters. However, in many cases, they are only trained for a few days or a couple weeks before being sent to your area. So, when the adjuster arrives at your property ask him if he is a temporary adjuster. If he is, you know up front that you may have a potential problem with the scope of your damages, and the amount of the estimate.

Remember that the estimate that any adjuster writes for your damages IS ONLY AN ESTIMATE. IT IS NOT A CONTRACT TO REPAIR YOUR PROPERTY. The chances are overwhelming that you will not be able to find a contractor to repair your property for the amount of the estimate. This is because materials and labor prices rapidly increase after a storm because of supply and demand. I don't know of any estimating software used by adjusters that takes into account the rapid increase in repair costs in an area that has suffered a catastrophe.

Remember that <u>nowhere in your policy</u> does it say that you have to get two or three estimates for repairs. Get the restoration contractor of your choice, not the choice of the insurance company. If you agree to use the insurance company's approved contractor, that's your decision. Finding contractors in the wake of a hurricane is sometimes a real challenge.

Most insurance companies want a preliminary estimate so that they can set their reserves. This is important for the insurance company because they have to set aside money to pay claims, and they want the amounts they set aside to be as accurate as possible. If they set aside too little money, the insurance regulators for each state get mad at them. If they set aside to much money, that adversely affects their investment income.

Most insurance companies also want to pay claims as soon as possible. So, if they get a preliminary estimate from the adjuster, they can issue an initial payment to their policyholder. That helps you, the policyholder, begin repairs sooner. Most people don't have tens of thousands of dollars just sitting around that they can use to hire contractors to repair their property, and then wait for the insurance company to reimburse them. Most contractors need money up front to begin repairs, as they have to buy materials before they begin repairs. They need the insurance payment to be made quickly to get the process started.

The best possible scenario for getting your claim paid more quickly is to have the adjuster and your contractor meet at your property and inspect it together. That way, they can agree on the scope of the damages right then. Later, when they both write an estimate, they can negotiate an agreed estimate based on their earlier agreement on the scope. You won't believe how much time this cuts out of your claim if it works.

Let me tell you about claims adjusters after Katrina and Rita. I was working as a Claims Supervisor. I did a few really large losses in New Orleans, but then my employer needed me to help with supervision. The field adjusters sent their reports to us in the home office, and we made sure they were accurate before sending them along to the Claims Departments at various insurance companies.

The field adjusters working out of the Catastrophe Offices down at the Gulf Shores area got assigned hundreds of claims each. There are only so many hours in a day, so frustration can set in very quickly for field adjusters.

First, they have to drive to the loss location. Many times the street signs and road signs have been blown away, so just finding the location is a challenge. When I worked Hurricane Andrew in Miami in 1992, we had to take detailed street maps and just count streets to find a house. All of the signs were gone.

Next, they have to try to meet the insured at the location. Many times, the homeowners were not there when the adjuster arrived…either they had evacuated to another town or state, or just had trouble getting back home. Cell phone towers were down so the adjusters couldn't call the insured even if they wanted to.

Next, they have to inspect the property. Hopefully, it's not raining. Hopefully, the roof is not too high for the ladder they carry with them. Hopefully, the roof is not too steep to walk on. Hopefully, the owner doesn't have a mean dog.

Next come the photos. Let me tell you how hard it is to keep photos straight when you're inspecting ten houses a day, six days a week.

It's real hard. Really, reeeeeealy hard.

Next, you have to make a diagram of the building and take really good notes on the damage.

Now, sometime you have to stop inspecting buildings and go back to your hotel room and start writing estimates.

Unfortunately, some adjusters will inspect dozens of properties before they begin writing estimates. It's nearly impossible to remember a house you looked at a month ago and try to write an accurate estimate. Most of the time, it's a challenge to remember what you did two days ago.

But the other way of doing it…inspect a few, write the estimate and report, inspect a few more…is just as time consuming as the other way. This is why some policyholders had to wait weeks and months before they could get an adjuster just to inspect their property..

So, even though it's terrible to have to wait weeks or months for your claim to be paid, there actually is a logical reason why the process takes so long in the aftermath of a major hurricane.

Turn in the book to Chapter Twelve, "Don't be in a Hurry." Do what it says.

Read Chapter Twenty Three, "Mold Claims."

# CHAPTER TWENTY NINE

# RECORDED STATEMENTS

I've taken hundreds of recorded statements over the years, and I know all of the tricks. People are so trusting, and will usually cooperate with the requests of someone they consider to be "official." Adjusters and claims examiners usually get that kind of deference from people, and I've never understood why. It probably has to do with the reason I wrote this book, which is that most people don't know much about their insurance policy and the claims process. They defer to the ones who know about it, and the ones who control the checkbooks.

Recorded statements are a normal part of the claims process. Claims adjusters usually like to get a recorded statement from all the parties in the loss early in the claims process. That way, the details of the claim are still fresh in everyone's minds, and can be documented more accurately. Don't be nervous about being recorded.

If the claims adjuster calls and requests a recorded statement over the telephone, politely tell him that you prefer to meet with him in person. The best scenario for you would be to meet the adjuster at your attorney's office, and give the recorded statement in the presence of the attorney. Even uncooperative or moody adjusters seem to be on their best behavior in the presence of an attorney.

Why am I so adamant about this?

You are not qualified to determine if you are at fault in a liability loss. Your liability is not for you to decide. If you give a statement in which you admit and accept fault and liability, it could prejudice your legal rights. It could bar you from recovery from the other party if the other party was even partially at fault. This is a very serious legal issue.

**Business Owners**: your employees may be required to give recorded statement in an insurance claim. For example, your employee was driving a company vehicle and had an accident with property damage and bodily injury to others. Likely the adjusters from both insurance companies will want to get a recorded statement.

**DO NOT ALLOW your employees to give a recorded statement to any adjuster unless they are in the presence of your attorney.**

Why? The reason is the same as before.

Your employee is not qualified to determine if he or she is at fault in a liability loss. If the employee gives a statement in which he or she admits and accepts fault and liability, it could prejudice your legal rights. It could bar you from recovery from the other party if the other party was even partially at fault. Once again, this is a serious legal issue in which hundreds of thousands of dollars could be at stake. A large insurance judgment over your policy limits could bankrupt you and close your business.

If the insurance adjuster or examiner only does recorded statements by phone, simply have the adjuster do a three-way conference call with you and your attorney.

On an in-person interview, the adjuster will have his portable tape recorder with which he will record the interview. You should also bring a portable tape recorder and tape the interview for your own protection. You can buy a hand-sized cassette recorder at any electronics store or discount department store…even major drug store chains for less than $40.00. They use standard cassette tapes and batteries. The microcassette recorders work great, too, and cost about the same. Make sure that you have plenty of fresh batteries and a few cassette tapes with you at the interview.

When the adjuster is recording your statement, don't OFFER any information. Answer the question that he asked, and no more. If he asks a "yes or no" question, answer without more details.

Remember that some questions do not deserve an answer.

Have you ever been in an interview, or some social situation, and someone asked you a question that made you uncomfortable? And you ANSWERED the question so they didn't think you were impolite? Then later you hated yourself for being a doormat?

People feel a need to be nice. Adjusters take advantage of people's need to be nice. Adjusters know that most people will answer whatever questions seem reasonable, even if the question is not relevant to the claim. <u>Personal questions that do not have relevance to your claim should not be answered.</u> Questions about your income, or asking for your Social Security number, may not be relevant to the claim. Questions about your income, for example, are not appropriate unless you are making a claim for lost wages.

One of the reasons that adjusters ask for your Social Security number is so they can look you up on a database called Insurance Service Office (ISO) Claimsearch. If you want to see what the Claimsearch homepage looks like, go to: <u>https://claimsearch.iso.com/index.asp</u>

Claimsearch is a searchable database that shows if you've ever had an insurance claim before. With your Social Security number, adjusters and claims examiners can call up all the data about you…WITHOUT YOUR PERMISSION.

If there's a question that the adjuster asks that you don't feel comfortable answering, politely reply "I'd rather not answer that question." Sometimes adjusters ask inappropriate questions. Make sure that the adjuster sticks to the details of the accident or loss. If you're in an attorney's office at the time of the recorded statement, he'll help the adjuster stay on track.

My belief is that you, the policyholder or claimant, should record <u>every</u> telephone conversation and face-to-face conversation that you have with <u>anyone</u> about your claim.  The same electronics stores that sell the cassette recorders will stock a "pick-up" microphone that plugs into your cassette recorder and has a suction cup that sticks to your telephone handset. The quality of the sound is usually quite good.

I'm not suggesting for a moment that you should do something illegal or unethical. You need to check your state's statutes and laws about recording conversations. Some states do not allow it unless both parties give consent. Some states allow it if only one of the parties is aware that the conversation is being recorded. I've posted the law about recording conversations in the Forms button at my website.

**Know the law, and know your rights.**

Don't be surprised if some people refuse to have their conversations recorded. That doesn't mean that you should cave in to their lack of cooperation. <u>You should insist on the recording, or politely refuse to speak with that person.</u> But, it should tell you something about that person if he or she refuses to be recorded.

Be in control of when and where you accept phone calls about your claim. I've seen some adjusters that try to keep the insured off balance by making calls at unusual times, like early morning or late night. If you're not ready to record the call when the phone rings, tell the person that it's not convenient to speak right then and make an appointment to call him back. <u>Always keep your appointments</u>.

I can imagine that some of you reading this chapter think that this author is some sort of paranoid kook. <u>Please let me assure you that I am</u>. But I've seen countless situations in which an adjuster took a recorded statement, and then wrote a statement summary that wasn't anything like the information on the tape. I've seen police officers fill out an accident report, and describe the accident completely wrongly. I've seen court testimony where the adjuster and the insured are questioned about an incident, and their stories are completely different.

Recordings of conversations put all of that to rest.

After you have a problem with a person who lies to you, or lies about you, it's too late to record them then.

The old adage is, "better safe than sorry." Sorry can cost you thousands of dollars.

**CHAPTER THIRTY**

# APPRAISAL CLAUSE

What if, after all you've done, you and your adjuster/insurance company are at an impasse on the value of your property? It's now time to invoke the Appraisal Clause in your insurance policy. The Appraisal Clause is usually found under the Heading "Conditions" and/or "What to do after a loss."

**HERE'S A REALLY IMPORTANT TIP!!!** You don't have to wait until you're hopelessly deadlocked with the adjuster or appraiser to invoke the Appraisal Clause. You can do it any time. I'm not suggesting that you become uncooperative. But occasionally, I talk to people who are having real difficulties with their adjuster or insurance company. Taking the claim to Appraisal sometimes stops all the drama.

Appraisal Clause is meant to be the method for determining disputed values. Appraisal cannot be used to determine what is covered. That is for a court of law to decide. If you have dispute with the company on whether or not something is covered, then you must file a lawsuit against your insurer to get that coverage determination.

Here's what the Appraisal Clause reads in the CP0010 Building and Personal Property Coverage Form.

"If we and you disagree on the value of the property or the amount of loss, either may make written demand for an appraisal of the loss. In this event, each party will select a competent and impartial appraiser. The two appraisers will select an umpire. If they cannot agree, either may request that selection be made by a judge of a court having jurisdiction. The appraisers will state separately the value of the property and amount of loss. If they fail to agree, they will submit their differences to the umpire. A decision agreed to by any two will be binding.
Each party will:
a. pay its chosen appraiser, and
b. Bear the other expenses of the appraisal and umpire equally."

Notice that there are NO specific time limits in the Clause. Your policy may vary. Read your policy.

The appraisers can still negotiate and reach an agreed amount of the damages. But, if they cannot agree, the case goes to the umpire. Then, if any two parties agree to the amount of the loss, that amount becomes the claim amount.
My recommendation, in the event of an appraisal, is to call a Claims Consultant (LIKE ME!), or a public adjusting company in your area to find an appraiser. A Claims Consultant or a PA are the best qualified claims experts I can think of to be able to evaluate and appraise a dispute like this. The Claims Consultant and the PA know insurance policies, know the Appraisal Clause, and know property values. The Claims Consultant or the PA are the perfect choice for helping you prove the values of the property of your claim.

## CHAPTER THIRTY ONE

# DIMINISHED VALUE

Insurance companies really hate this topic. Let's explore it, and then you'll know how it could affect you if you have any kind of a collision loss.

In this chapter, I'm going to refer to all cars, trucks, motorcycles, boats, RVs, anything you can drive, as "vehicles."

Vehicles of every type depreciate. For those of you not familiar with that term, it simply means that vehicles lose their value over time. Most everyone has had the experience of buying a car for a certain price, and then finding out five years later that, when you try to sell the car, it's worth far less than when you bought it.

Chapter Twenty One deals with depreciation. Don't forget to read it.

Remember that depreciation is affected by time, but also by the condition of the vehicle. If you keep your vehicle in perfect condition, it will depreciate more slowly than a vehicle that's not in such pristine condition. But it's still going to depreciate.

Even if your vehicle is maintained perfectly, the value of your vehicle will shrink if it has been in an accident.

Diminished value (DV) is the loss in market value that happens when a vehicle is damaged and then repaired. Think about this example: if you were looking at two identical vehicles with the idea of buying one of them...and one had been wrecked and repaired, even extremely well repaired, and the other vehicle had no damage...and they were the same price...which one would you want to buy? You'd probably choose the one with no damage.

Next question: how much of a discount off the selling price would you have to get to give serious consideration to buying the car that had the damage? Well, that discount is, in essence, the "diminished value" of that repaired vehicle.

The principle in the law of Diminished Value has a long and generally accepted history. That hasn't stopped the insurance industry, however. The insurance companies have been denying DV claims for years, and they'll continue to deny claims for DV. <u>Some insurance companies LIE about the law.</u> Let me show you how.

In the State of Georgia, there was a landmark court case about DV called Mabry v. State Farm. On November 28, 2001 the case was handed down from the Georgia Supreme Court. The decision stated that ALL insurance companies doing business in the State of Georgia had to pay diminished value as a part of the collision claim. The parties IN THIS CASE agreed to use a formula to calculate the diminished value, called the "17C formula."

The "17C formula" was ONLY MEANT for the two parties in that particular case. There is nothing in the ruling that directs EVERYBODY to use the "17C formula." The formula was crafted by the insurance companies to lower the amount they would have to pay in any DV loss.

These days, many insurance companies flatly refuse to pay DV. If they do give it consideration, they will try to use the "17C formula" in the calculation of the claim. They might even try to refer to the Georgia Supreme Court case as their precedent.

If your vehicle is damaged in an accident, the insurance company owes you money for Diminished Value. There is no state in the USA where this is NOT TRUE.

The foremost experts in the nation about Diminished Value are here in the Atlanta area. Their business is called Collision Claim Associates, Inc., in Cumming, Georgia. They serve clients in all 50 states. Their website is crammed full of extremely important information about Diminished Value, and how you can collect every dollar that you're entitled to collect. They offer a FREE DV claim review at the site. If you want a full written report, they charge a fee for that.

I strongly recommend these guys!! Their website address is: www.collisionclaims.com

There is another very serious issue that I wrote briefly about in Chapter 23 of my first book. That is the safety of your repaired vehicle. This safety issue directly affects Diminished Value.

In the automotive parts industry, there is something called "Aftermarket Parts." Depending on whom you ask, these parts are equal, better or worse than the Original Equipment Manufacturer parts. These are parts not necessarily manufactured to Original Equipment Manufacturer (OEM) specifications. They are NOT OEM parts. In most cases, they are inferior parts, and cost much less than OEM parts. One of the reasons they are cheaper is that they are not subject to the same crash testing procedures as OEM and therefore are not as safe.

The auto manufacturers get safety certification from the US Federal Government for their products. That means that every part that goes into a vehicle has to pass strict government standards.

Aftermarket parts may be interchangeable in repairs, but they are NOT OEM parts.

That means that, if you repair your vehicle with aftermarket parts, it would not pass a Federal inspection for safety.

If you plan on reselling or trading your car, you should seriously consider only using OEM parts. These days, anyone with an internet connection and the vehicle identification number can check your vehicle's damage repair history. All they have to do is go to www.carfax.com . Body shops and insurance companies report damages to Carfax, and it goes into their database.

The trade-in value of your car, repaired with aftermarket parts, could be significantly diminished. Also, using non-OEM parts to repair a leased car could cost you all or part of your security deposit, since you won't be returning the vehicle to the dealer in the same condition as when you took delivery of the vehicle.

Insurance companies don't really care about your safety. For the most part, the insurance companies will encourage you to use aftermarket parts to repair your vehicle after a wreck. In fact, some insurance companies state that they will only pay for repairs done with aftermarket parts.

A few insurance companies, such as Chubb Insurance, actually encourage their policyholders to use OEM parts, while not charging them a penalty. The Travelers even ran a cute TV ad about a rattlesnake that had a baby's plastic rattle tied to his tail.

Insurance claims are designed to return your property to its pre-loss condition, if possible. If your vehicle was an OEM vehicle prior to the accident, then the ONLY WAY to return your vehicle to its pre-loss condition is to use OEM parts.

Anything else is allowing the insurance company to rip you off!!

If your vehicle had been damaged before, and you're now replacing aftermarket parts with more aftermarket parts, there's not a lot that can be argued about the safety issue. I'd still recommend that you replace the damaged aftermarket parts with OEM in order to return your car to its safest condition. It might cost you some money over and above the insurance payment, but you'd be safer.

So, in ANY accident…whether you're at fault, or some one else is at fault, INSIST on OEM parts for the repair of your vehicle. Fight for it! Call the State Department of Insurance and file a complaint. Call the local Consumer radio or TV talk show and tell your story. Call the local newspaper and try to get them to do a story about your experience. Fight and WIN!!

CHAPTER THIRTY TWO

# UNFAIR CLAIMS PRACTICES

Insurance companies refused to settle thousands of claims after Hurricanes Katrina and Rita and showed America just what Unfair Claims Practices can look like. But Unfair Claims Practices happen in more than just hurricanes losses. Insurance companies deny and delay claims on a very regular basis.

What do you do when your insurance company drags its feet and will not settle your claim? How do you tell what actions are just simply annoyingly poor customer service, and what actions violate the law?

How do you know if your insurance company is treating you fairly and lawfully after you have filed an insurance claim?

Every state has Unfair Claims Practices regulations to protect policyholders and claimants from being abused by insurance companies in the claims process.

A state regulator's primary task is protecting the interests of insurance consumers. Check with your state's Department of Insurance to find out the regulations in your state.

Let me give you some examples of Unfair Claims Practices:

* Attempting to settle a claim based on an application which the company changed without the insured's knowledge or permission. The simplest example of this is when an insurance company changes the date of the application. But it could be any information on the application that might be altered.

* Failing to act promptly after receiving information concerning an insurance claim. Many states require response within 15 days. When there's a storm like Katrina, you might have to wait weeks to meet your adjuster. But that might be an Unfair Claims Practice.

* Delaying a claim investigation by requiring unnecessary reports or documents which contain substantially the same information. Recently I witnessed a major well-known insurance company send a claim to their Special Investigations Unit (SUI), and then take recorded statements from the insureds...and then ask the insureds to submit to an Examination Under Oath. In my opinion, that was Unfair Claims Practice perpetrated by that insurance company.

* When applicable, failing to pay a claim quickly, fairly and equitably. Unethical insurance companies could just stonewall you by telling you it is still investigating your claim.

* Failing to promptly settle claims where liability is reasonably clear under one portion of the policy to influence settlements under any portion of the insurance policy coverage. For example, your auto insurer can't refuse to pay your bills under the medical coverage in your policy so you'll settle your uninsured motorist claim.

\* <u>Failing to promptly and clearly explain the policy or the law for either denying a claim or offering a compromise settlement.</u> If you get a denial letter for your claim, the letter should quote the policy language directly that applies. No quote, could be Unfair Claim Practice.

\* <u>Attempting to persuade insureds not to invoke and use the arbitration process.</u> Also, an insurance company is prevented from appealing almost all of the arbitration awards in favor of policyholders as a way to force a settlement of claims.

\* <u>Misrepresenting significant facts or insurance policy provisions.</u> Insurance companies sometimes deny claims on their misinterpretation of the policy. Then, it's up to you to change their minds.

.

\* <u>Refusing to tell an insured what is happening with a loss within a reasonable time after receiving a completed proof of loss statement.</u> Many policies require the insurance company to accept or deny the proof of loss within 30 days after receiving it. It's in your policy...read it.

\* <u>Denying claims without a reasonable loss investigation.</u> The problem comes with the definition of "reasonable." Still, insurers sometimes try to settle a claim using a "lowball settlement offer" without much investigation, just to see if they can make the claim go away.

\* <u>Offering very low settlements to encourage insureds to sue.</u> That would cause the length of time for a claim settlement to stretch out, possibly for years. The only ones who benefit from that delay are the insurance company...and the attorneys

 * <u>Settling claims for less than the amounts a reasonable person would expect.</u> Insurance companies regularly make "lowball offers" for settlements to their own policyholders as well as third-party claimants. The insurers will pay the LEAST amount of money in a settlement that the policyholders or claimants will accept...always. That's one way to maximize profits.

If you think that your insurance company examiner or adjuster is has committed an Unfair Claims Practices action, talk to that person's supervisor. If the situation doesn't improve or get entirely resolved, file a complaint with your state's insurance department.

## CHAPTER THIRTY THREE

# THE '59 VETTE

Occasionally, a claimant gets to look on with abject horror as the loss occurs. This was one of those times.

Mike is a successful businessman in a small town near Olympia, Washington. He decided to reward himself by purchasing a classic car. So, he spent many hours online looking for the perfect automobile.

He finally found his dream car in Southern California. It was a 1959 Corvette, all original, low mileage, matching vehicle numbers, never damaged, original white lacquer paint. Mike had the owner send him tons of photos and copies of the available documents. Mike didn't even travel to California to inspect the 'Vette in person. He agreed with the owner on a price of $68,000, and they completed their transaction.

The seller arranged for a custom car hauler to pick up the 'Vette and deliver it to Mike in Washington. The hauler was our insured with a Motor Truck Cargo policy. He picked up the car in Southern California and placed it on his trailer. The hauler secured the car and headed to Washington.

When he arrived, Mike warmly and excitedly met him. The hauler unchained the 'Vette from the trailer, got into the car and started the engine. The hauler put the shifter in reverse and prepared to back off the trailer. He cracked open the driver's door so he could look over his left shoulder while backing the trailer down the ramp.

But the hauler did not notice the trailer's vertical structural member so close to the car door as he backed up. The driver's door struck the structural member of the trailer with a sickening crunch. Mike watched in astonishment and horror as his dream car was damaged. The hauler finished getting the car off the trailer and sheepishly apologized. The driver's door now had a fist-sized hole in the door edge just below the door handle.

Later, the hauler told me by phone that if Mike had punched him in the nose he would have deserved it. But, the only violence that day was suffered by the 'Vette.

When I got the claim, I called Mike and arranged for the car to be appraised. The appraiser I used sent me an appraisal, but it was obvious that the appraiser had no experience with classic cars. The appraisal was written for about $3,500.00. I rejected it out of hand.

I considered our financial exposure as the insurer to be high. Here was a classic car worth $68,000 that had never been damaged in any way. There was a hole in a 40-year-old fiberglass door. A replacement door could be located, but then the car would cease to be original. That could have created a large diminished value loss.

Also, the original lacquer paint could not be matched. We could not just paint the door after repairs, for the door is in the middle of the car. The mismatched paint would be a glaring error. The entire car would have to be repainted.

I called Mike, the distraught owner. I asked him to take the car to a body shop of his choice and have the body shop write a correct estimate. He said he would.

A few days later, Mike's chosen body shop sent me an estimate right around $15,000. I discussed it with Mike and he was satisfied that it was a comprehensive estimate encompassing all possible repairs. I sent him a Release form and we paid the claim.

Mike admitted to being somewhat stunned by this settlement. He said he thought he would have to fight with me over the repairs based on the first low estimate. But what I could not reveal to Mike is that I thought our financial exposure to be over $30,000, so I thought that I was making a tremendous deal at only $15,000 for my client, the insurance company.

Mike drives his gorgeous 'Vette on weekends, but never in the rain.

CHAPTER THIRTY FOUR

# JUST A SONG BEFORE I GO

If you're as old as I am, you'd remember that this chapter title is taken from the last cut on side two of the album "Deja Vu," by Crosby, Stills, Nash and Young.

The last line of the song is very applicable to the theme of this entire book, which is taking control of your insurance claims, and adding hundred or even thousands more dollars to your claim settlements.

"Just a song before I go,
A lesson to be learned,
Traveling twice the speed of sound
It's easy to get burned."

In the insurance claims process, many claimants and policyholders get burned because they don't know how to submit their claims properly. When the insurance companies control the flame, so to speak, you'll be fortunate not to get burned. But by reading this book and using the strategies for yourself, you've turned a fire hose loose on them!

Here are a few things that may have been talked about in other chapters, but still need to be reinforced here…just to make sure that you do them.

## PROPERTY CLAIMS

### Repair Work

No contractor or vendor gets to do any repair work without a signed contract.

### Waiver of Lien

A Waiver if Lien form is a simple legal form. The company or individual who signs the form agrees that the payment they receive is payment in full, and they give up their right to claim a mechanic's lien on your assets for the amount of money listed in the form.

Mechanic's Liens are troublesome to say the least. They happen when a vendor or contractor does work and doesn't get paid for it. That vendor or contractor goes to court and slaps a lien on your property for the amount that the Court awards him. That ties up your title or deed, and you can't sell your property without paying the Mechanic's Lien first.

The Waiver of Lien prevents the vendor or contractor from filing a lien against your property.

It's customary for a contractor or subcontractor to sign one of these forms EVERY TIME THEY GET PAID. That means that if you had a contractor working or repairing your business for three months, he would need to sign at least three separate Waiver forms…one every month he got paid.

In property losses, you may have contractors or subcontractors that are performing repairs for you. Make SURE that you have ALL persons who will get paid for repairs sign a Waiver of Lien form BEFORE you sign the check. (or before the bank signs the check if you have a lender managing a repair escrow account.)

This should be a non-negotiable issue. Either the vendor signs the Waiver of Lien form, or he doesn't get paid. Period.

You'll find a simple Waiver of Lien form at the website in the Forms Section. Simply download a copy and fill in the blanks.

### Sworn Statement in Proof of Loss

You'll find one of these forms at the website also. I'm going to call it a "Proof."

The Proof is only meant to settle the AMOUNT of a claim. It is NEVER used to settle whether certain damage is covered or not covered. Coverage questions are settled in a court of law. If your insurance company denies coverage on your damages, you may have to file suit to get a determination by a judge on coverage.

The Proof is a form signed by the Insured, between the Insured and the insurance company. This is a two party form only. The Proof is mentioned in your policy. Many insurance companies require this form to be signed before they release any money in settlement of a claim. Many times the insurance company will allow partial Proofs to be signed by the insured when they pay advances.

If you had a fire at your business, you would likely have a Building loss as well as Business Personal Property (Contents) losses. Your Contents loss might be ready to settle before the building loss is ready. In that case, the insurance company would likely accept a partial Proof in the amount of the Contents settlement so that you'd not have to wait for your money.

Some times, there is a dispute between the Insured and the insurance company on the amount of the settlement. In order to prevent or stop the insurance company from stalling or delaying payment of the claim indefinitely, the insured (THAT'S YOU!) can sign a Proof and send it to the insurance company. The Homeowners insurance policy (HO3) usually gives the company 60 days to respond. Business insurance policies (CP 0010 form) only give the insurance company 30 days to respond.

Be very careful as you fill out the form. If you have a Public Adjuster, ask him to help you complete the form. If not, simply be careful yourself.

If you have a lienholder on your property, do not fail to disclose the name and address of the lienholder. The insurance company will then issue a payment with your name and the lienholder listed on the check.

Remember, you should not sign a form of ANY KIND without your attorney reviewing the form first.

You should ALWAYS send the signed Proof to the insurance company by certified mail, return receipt requested.

Once the insurance company receives the form, they have to do one of two things:

1. Accept the form and pay the claim.
2. Reject the form and tell you why.

Choice #2 is very serious. The insurance company is in danger of an Unfair Claims Practices violation and a fine from the Department of Insurance of your state. I'm not saying that rejection of a Proof is an automatic violation. I'm just saying that they'd better have a really good reason for the rejection.

Either way, you're moving the claim toward completion.

## CASUALTY CLAIMS

These can be:

-Auto liability
-General liability
-Workers Compensation

I could go on for hours and pages about the many ways that liability claims are settled. However, this is a book about claims strategies. I'm not going to include recent court cases and impress you with my claims knowledge. The best advice I can offer here in this book is:

1. If you are in a situation in which you MIGHT be liable for damages to someone, consult your attorney IMMEDIATELY. I realize that the insurance policy MIGHT cover this loss and the insurance company MIGHT have to provide a defense for you. But you need to protect yourself FIRST. Your attorney will be happy to work with an insurance defense attorney if and when one is appointed by the insurance company. But there are defense strategies that need to be discussed BEFORE the insurance company gets your claim.

2. In negotiations, start high…negotiate down slowly when trying to maximize a settlement. Start low and negotiate slowly upward when trying to minimize a settlement.

3. The generally accepted method of completing a liability claim in which you are the Claimant is the other party's insurance company will ask you to sign a Release form. A Release form basically states that you accept the conditions of the settlement and that you give up your right to pursue any further damages from the other party. NEVER, EVER sign a Release form of ANY TYPE without your attorney reviewing it FIRST. Once it's signed it's too late.

4. Usually, when you are the Defendant (the person liable) and the other guy is the Claimant (the person with damages) the insurance company will defend you and negotiate on your behalf. Your insurance company will get the Claimants to sign as restrictive a Release form as they will agree to sign.

I'll deal with some liability issues in my monthly newsletter. There are also archived articles at the website about liability.

\* \* \* \* \* \* \*

Settling the claim is the reward at the end of your hard work. You will learn a lot about human behavior, negotiation, law, insurance contracts, repair costs, and just people in general through this process of getting your claim paid. But, if you have followed the strategies in this book to the best of your abilities, you should be able to see the tangible evidence of your work when you receive the checks from the insurance company. It should be hundreds or thousands of dollars more than you would have received without your good work.

Here's wishing all my best to you. I am so honored that you have purchased my book. Thank you! I hope we have a long and mutually profitable relationship.

If you have a story about how this book helped you, I'd love to hear that story. Please go to the website and leave me an email message. I'll cheer for you when I read it. With your permission, I might even publish YOUR story in the newsletter!!

# APPENDIX

This book has been written to be a book of strategy, showing you how to take control of your claim and collect hundreds or thousands of dollars MORE than you would if you were not in control.

It is my greatest desire that you will use the strategies found in this book. I purposefully did not try to fill the back pages of the book with forms, shrunken down to fit the format size of this book.

All the forms you will need will be found in the Resource section on my website. All you have to do is click on the form you need, and you can print the form in Word format. The forms are FREE!!

The website address is:

www.insurance-claim-secrets.com

At the website, you will also find a place to sign up for my <u>FREE</u> monthly newsletter. That newsletter will give you terrific information not just about claims, but topics like:

- Top Ten biggest insurance ripoffs
- How to save money on auto insurance
- How to save money on homeowners insurance
- How to save money on business insurance
- Super deals on 3-day and 4-day driveaway vacations
- How to save THOUSANDS on your taxes each year!
- How to buy life insurance and NOT GET RIPPED OFF!!
- Identity Theft!!
- How to manage deductibles
- How to fight traffic tickets and win most every time
- What about liability umbrella policies?
- Getting your Last Will and Testament written FREE!
- How to buy renter's insurance
- How to take a home inventory of your contents
- Flood insurance
- Secrets about business insurance policies
- Beware of body shop ripoffs
- How to find a great insurance agent
- Investing and the Rule of 72
- Financial Planners, not insurance agents
- Boat, Motorcycle, Snowmobile, ATV insurance
- And MUCH, MUCH MORE!!!

Plus, see the newest and freshest monthly information on handling your money and protecting your assets.

If you only get ONE great idea from my monthly newsletter, it could save you THOUSANDS!

There will also be links to other websites that will add SUPER VALUE to your life.

Remember, I will NEVER share my newsletter subscriber list with ANYONE. THERE IS NO COST...unsubscribe at any time. We'll LOVE having you as part of the family while you're with us, and miss you if you leave!

## Get Help from your State Department of Insurance

There is no Federal Department of Insurance. Thankfully, the states each set their own regulations and statutes for insurance. Each state has its own Department of Insurance where consumers can go to obtain assistance dealing with problems they're having with insurance companies.

Many times in this book, I've recommended that if you do not get satisfaction from the insurance company or the claims adjuster in getting your claim paid, you should contact your state's Department of Insurance.

There's a SUPER helpful website developed by the National Association of Insurance Commissioners. At that site, there is a map of the US and its territories. Click on your state, and it takes you right to your state's Department of Insurance website.

The website address is:

http://www.naic.org/state_web_map.htm

A word of encouragement here. I know people have a need to be nice, and try and get along with everyone. That's really an admirable quality. It stops being so admirable when the insurance company claims examiner or the claims adjuster are refusing to help you collect all of the money you are entitled to collect.

When your adjuster or the claims examiner at the insurance company "drags their feet" or "digs in their heels" and will not compromise in the processing of your claim, it's time to call in the people that regulate them…if only to make sure that they are not violating a state law.

After all, your tax dollars are funding this very valuable state governmental unit. And, I've found that the state departments of insurance usually favor the consumer, not the insurance companies.

The Department of Insurance is there to help you solve problems in your claims process.

USE THEM!!!

For those of you that might not have access to the website, here is a list of all of the state Insurance Departments.

## Department of Insurance for all US States and Territories

### ALASKA
Alaska Division of Insurance

550 West 7$^{th}$ Avenue, Suite 1560
Anchorage, AL 99501-3567
907-269-7900
Fax 907-269-7910

### ALABAMA
Alabama Department of Insurance
201 Monroe Street
Montgomery, AL 36104
334-269-3550
Fax 334-241-4192

### CALIFORNIA
California Department of Insurance
300 Capitol Mall, Suite 1700
Sacramento, CA 95814
916-492-3500
Fax 916-445-6552

### COLORADO
Colorado Division of Insurance
1560 Broadway, Suite 850
Denver, CO 80202
303-894-7499
Fax 303-894-7455

## ARKANSAS
Arkansas Department of Insurance
12000 West 3$^{rd}$ Street
Little Rock, AR 72201
501-371-2600
Fax 501-371-2629

## AMERICAN SAMOA
Office of the Governor
American Samoa Government
Pago Pago, AS 96799
684-633-4116
Fax 684-633-2269

## ARIZONA
Arizona Department of Insurance

2910 North 44$^{th}$ Street, Suite 220
Phoenix, AZ 85018
602-912-8400
Fax 602-912-8452

## FLORIDA
Department of Financial Services
State Capitol, Plaza Level Eleven
Tallahassee, FL 32399
850-413-2806
Fax 850-413-2950

## GEORGIA
Georgia Department of Insurance
2 Martin Luther King Jr. Drive
Floyd Building, 704 West Tower
Atlanta, GA 30334
404-656-2056
Fax 404-656-4688

## CONNECTICUT
Connecticut Department of
Insurance
153 Market Street, 7$^{th}$ Floor
Hartford, CT 06103
860-297-3800
Fax 860-566-7410

## DISTRICT OF COLUMBIA
Department of Insurance
801 First Street, NE, Suite 701
Washington, DC 20002
202-727-8000
Fax 202-535-1196

## DELAWARE
Delaware Department of
Insurance
Rodney Building
841 Silver Lake Blvd.
Dover, Delaware
302-739-4251
Fax 302-739-5280

## IDAHO
Idaho Department of Insurance
700 West State Street, 3$^{rd}$ Floor
Boise, ID 83720
208-334-4250
Fax 208-334-4398

## ILLINOIS
Illinois Division of Insurance
320 W. Washington St., 4$^{th}$ Floor
Springfield, IL 62767

217-785-5516
217-524-6500

## GUAM
Department of Rev. & Taxation

Government of Guam

1240 Route 16
Barrigada, Guam 96913
671-635-1843
671-633-2643

## HAWAII
Hawaii Insurance Division

Dep't. of Consumer Affairs
335 Merchant Street, Room 213
Honolulu, HI 96811
808-586-2790
Fax 808-586-2806

## IOWA
Iowa Division of Insurance
330 E. Maple Street
Des Moines, IA 50319
515-281-5523
Fax 505-281-3059

## LOUISIANA
Louisiana Department of Insurance

1702 N. 3$^{rd}$ Street
Baton Rouge, LA 70802
225-342-5423
Fax 225-342-8622

## INDIANA
Indiana Department of
Insurance
311 W. Washington Street, Suite
300
Indianapolis, IN 46204

317-232-2385
Fax 317-232-5251

## KANSAS
Kansas Department of
Insurance
420 SW 9$^{th}$ Street
Topeka, KS 66612

785-296-3071
Fax 785-296-7805

## KENTUCKY
Kentucky Office of Insurance
215 W. Main Street
Frankfort, KY 40601
502-564-6027
Fax 502-564-1453

## MINNESOTA
Minnesota Department of
Commerce
85 7$^{th}$ Place East, Suite 500
St Paul, MN 55101
651-296-5769
Fax 651-282-2568

## MASSACHUSETTS
Division of Insurance

Commonwealth of Massachusetts
One South Station, 5<sup>th</sup> Floor
Boston, MA 02110
617-521-7794
Fax 617-521-7758

## MARYLAND

Maryland Insurance Administration
525 St. Paul Place
Baltimore, MD 21202
410-468-2090
410-468-2019

## MAINE
Maine Bureau of Insurance

State Office Building, Station 34
Augusta, ME 04333
207-624-8401
Fax 207-624-8599

## MICHIGAN
State of Michigan
Office of Financial
& Insurance Services
611 W. Ottawa, 3<sup>rd</sup> Floor
Lansing, MI 48909
517-373-0220
Fax 517-373-4870

## MISSOURI
Missouri Department of
Insurance
301 West High Street, Suite 530
Jefferson City, MO 65101

573-751-4126
Fax 573-751-1165

## NORTH MARIANA ISLANDS
Department of Insurance
Caller Box 10007 CK
Saipan, MP 96950
670-664-3000

## MISSISSIPPI
Mississippi Insurance
Department
501 North West Street
Jackson, MS 39205
601-359-3569
Fax 601-359-2474

## MONTANA
Montana Department of
Insurance
840 Helena Avenue
Helena, MT 59601

406-444-2040
406-444-3497

## NORTH CAROLINA
Department of Insurance
430 N. Salisbury Street
Raleigh, NC 27603
919-733-3058
Fax 919-733-6495

## NORTH DAKOTA
Department of Insurance

600 East Boulevard

Bismarck, ND 585505
701-328-2440
Fax 701-328-4880

## NEBRASKA
Nebraska Department of Insurance
Terminal Building, Suite 400
941 "O" Street
Lincoln, NE 68508
402-471-2201
Fax 402-471-4610

## NEW HAMPSHIRE
Department of Insurance

21 South Fruit Street, Suite 14
Concord, NH 03301
603-271-2261
Fax 603-271-1406

## NEW JERSEY
New Jersey Department of Insurance
20 West State Street, CN325

Trenton, NJ 08625
609-633-7667
Fax 609-984-5273

## NEVADA
Nevada Division of Insurance
788 Fairview Drive, Suite 300
Carson City, NV 89701
775-687-4270
Fax 775-687-3937

## NEW YORK
New York Department of
Insurance
One Commerce Plaza, Suite
1700
Albany, NY 12257
518-474-4567
Fax 518-473-4139

## OHIO
Ohio Department of Insurance
2100 Stella Court
Columbus, OH 43215

614-644-2658
Fax 614-644-3743

## OKLAHOMA
Oklahoma Department of
Insurance
2401 NW 23rd Street, Suite 28
Oklahoma City, OK 73107
405-521-2828
Fax 405-521-6635

## OREGON
Oregon Insurance Division
350 Winter Street NE, Room
440
Salem, OR 97301
503-947-7980
Fax 503-378-4351

## NEW MEXICO
Department of Insurance

PERA Building, 1200 Pasa de Peralta

Santa Fe, NM 87504
505-827-4601
Fax 505-476-0326

## PUERTO RICO
Puerto Rico Department of Insurance
1607 Ponce de Leon Avenue Stop 23
Santurce, Puerto Rico 00910
787-722-8686
Fax 787-722-4400

## RHODE ISLAND
Rhode Island Insurance Division
233 Richmond Street, Suite 233
Providence , RI 02903
401-222-5466
Fax 401-222-5475

## SOUTH CAROLINA
Department of Insurance

300 Arbor Lake Drive, Suite 1200
Columbia, SC 29202
00802
803-737-6227
Fax 803-737-6159

## SOUTH DAKOTA
South Dakota Division of Insurance
445 East Capitol Avenue, 1$^{st}$ Floor
Pierre, SD 57501
605-773-4104
Fax 605-773-5369

## PENNSYLVANIA
Pennsylvania Insurance Department
1426 Strawberry Square, 13$^{th}$ Floor
Harrisburg, PA 17120
717-783-0442
Fax 717-772-1969

## UTAH
Utah Department of Insurance
3110 State Office Building
Salt Lake City, UT 84114
801-538-3800
Fax 801-538-3829

## VIRGINIA
Virginia Bureau of Insurance
1300 East Main Street
Richmond, VA 23219
804-371-9694
Fax 804-371-9873

## VIRGIN ISLANDS
Division of Banking and Insurance
1131 King Street, Suite 101
Christiansted, St. Croix, VI

340-773-6449
Fax 340-773-4052

## VERMONT
Vermont Division of Insurance
89 Main Street, Drawer 20
Montpelier, VT 05620
802-828-3301
Fax 802-828-3306

## TENNESSEE
Tennessee Department of Insurance

Davy Crockett Tower, 5<sup>th</sup> Floor
500 James Robertson Parkway
Nashville, TN 37243
615-741-6007
Fax 615-532-6934

## TEXAS
Texas Department of Insurance

333 Guadalupe Street
Austin, TX 78701
512-463-6464
Fax 512-475-2005

## WASHINGTON
Washington Dept. of Insurance

5000 Capitol Way
Tumwater, WA 98501

360-725-7000
Fax 360-586-3109

## WISCONSIN
Wisconsin Department of
Insurance
125 S. Webster, GEF III, 2<sup>nd</sup> Fl.
Madison, WI 53702
608-267-1233
Fax 608-261-8579

## WEST VIRGINIA
West Virginia Insurance Commission

1124 Smith Street
Charleston, WV 25301
304-558-3354
Fax 304-558-0412

## WYOMING
Wyoming Department of
Insurance
Herschler Building
122 W. 25<sup>th</sup> Street, 3<sup>rd</sup> East
Cheyenne, WY 82002
307-777-7401
Fax 307-777-5895

# ABOUT THE AUTHOR

Russell D. Longcore has an international insurance claim consulting practice in Atlanta, Georgia, USA. In his 38-plus year career in insurance, he has handled claims as simple as a water leak in a home, and as complicated as multi-million dollar commercial property and liability losses. He is also a professional Appraiser and Umpire for Insurance Appraisal Clause disputes, and expert witness in court cases.

Russell began his career in claims in 1992 as a "storm trooper" after Hurricane Andrew. He has worked every American hurricane since. Because of Russell's background as an insurance agent and as a commercial builder, he has been able to rocket to the very pinnacle of his profession. Russell was an Executive General Adjuster in the Global Technical Division for the world's largest independent adjusting company, headquartered in Atlanta, just prior to founding his claims consulting practice.

Russell is the author of the hot-selling book entitled *"Insurance Claim Secrets REVEALED!"*

The book shows consumers how to take control of their insurance claims, and add hundreds or even thousands more dollars to their claim settlements. The book hit Number One in two categories at Amazon.com in October 2007, and has been Number One continuously ever since, nearly five years! Russ was also nominated for "2008 Author of The Year" by the Georgia Writers Association for this book.

This book was also a Finalist in USA Book News "Best Book Awards 2008."

He also owns Abigail Morgan Austin Publishing Company. Russell can be reached at:

Abigail Morgan Austin Publishing Company
1750 Powder Springs Road, Suite 190
Marietta, Georgia 30064
Website: www.insurance-claim-secrets.com

"This book is an easily readable, highly informative insider's view of the claims process. Don't file your next claim without reading it."
Tim Ryles, Ph.D.,
Former Georgia Commissioner of Insurance

Russell D. Longcore

# INSURANCE CLAIM SECRETS REVEALED!

Take Control of Your Insurance Claims! Add Hundreds or Even Thousands More Dollars to Your Claim Settlement!

Russ is also President and Founder of Masterpiece Energy LLC, an energy company that markets residential and commercial electricity and natural gas in multiple US states. Learn more at: www.MasterpieceEnergy.com

Russ is also Founder and Editor of a large Internet article directory at: www.SuperArticleDirectory.com . The directory has over 61,000 authors and over 750,000 articles posted. Writing and posting articles to promote your hobby or business is a very effective way to build sales and establish yourself as an expert. And, it is FREE!

Russ owns: www.InsuranceQuoteHQ.com . Get a quote on the insurance you are going to buy. The service is FREE and you will get insurance agents competing for your business in your area, no matter where you are.

Russ owns the domain registry and web hosting website at: www.BigGenieDomains.com.  Let the Big Genie host your website! But before you have a website, you must secure your domain name. The Big Genie will help you find that special name for that special website!

Here is the best example. Most people are afraid that if they submit a claim to their insurance company, their policy might be cancelled. It happens regularly, doesn't it? Well, if the insurance companies were loyal to you, they would continue collecting premium from you to make up for the claim they paid for you. But instead, you get cancelled.

You might like your agent. He might be one of your best friends. But that doesn't matter at claim time.

The Internet has made it very easy and simple to get quotes. And, you can get quotes from multiple companies for any kind of policy known to man.

Enter the words "insurance quote" in any search engine and you will see thousands of vendors, all eager to give you quotes.

**So...how do you choose which insurance quote service to use? Are they all alike?**

NO...NO...NO!!!

I have visited dozens and dozens of these websites, and I noticed a common flaw.

**They don't think like a claims adjuster. They think like sales people.**

The other quote websites seem to be all about the lowest cost insurance quotes. Now, don't get me wrong. I like low prices as much as the next guy.

But, isn't there usually a difference between lowest price and best value?

Insurance is a service, not really a product. So, great customer service should be near the top of your list of benefits for buying insurance. But you should not be only concerned with great customer service when you're buying your policy.

**You should be MOSTLY concerned with the service you get when you have a loss.** After all, insurance is all about keeping promises.

You enter into a contract with the insurance company. You promise certain things, like paying your premium. They promise to pay your claim if your loss is covered.

But most people I've ever talked to don't know the first thing about how to handle an insurance claim. That puts them...**YOU**...entirely at the mercy of the insurance company and the insurance adjuster.

Many times, people who have had a loss are on the raw edge of emotion. Isn't is natural to be fearful in a situation where you don't feel you're in control...where you don't know what will happen next, and you're scared you'll be "ripped off?" Most everyone has heard a story from a relative or friend about an insurance claim that went badly.

People like that **need solid advice and a strategy** on what to do to get their claim paid.

They need to **understand the claims process completely** so that they are not at the mercy of the insurance company, the claims adjuster and the claims examiner.

They need to be **paid every dollar** that they are entitled to collect.
They need to have **peace of mind knowing that their claim was handled correctly.**

Every policy you can buy will have a section that tells you what you must do when you have a loss and want to file a claim. But, the policy NEVER tells you HOW to file your claim. The policy NEVER tells you about the "claims process."

**Why?**

It's simple, really. If you don't know where to turn for help in the claims process, you will naturally turn to the insurance company for help. If you allow them to help you prepare and submit your claim, you can be certain that you will NOT COLLECT every dollar you should. If the insurance company controls the claims process, **YOU LOSE!**

**The "devil is in the details" of the claims process.** The insurance companies all rely on the fact that their policyholders don't know the claims process. That lack of knowledge helps the insurance companies hold down claim settlement amounts. That increases their profits...but at your expense.

So, what can you do?

**You must become at least as claims-conscious as price-conscious.**

In 2009, I started an insurance quote service at: www.InsuranceQuoteHQ.com . At IQHQ, you can get insurance quotes for any kind of insurance imaginable. And, when you submit the form for your quote, you will receive competitive quotes from many companies, not just one or two.
We quote in North America, Europe and the UK.

Here's one of the great benefits...**this service is FREE!** You have **NO COST...NO OBLIGATION...NOT EVER!!**

So, go ahead and confidently get the best insurance quote and lowest price on your insurance!

**And I'll help you become claims-conscious! Here's how...**

I recommend taking a four-step approach:

1. Go to: www.InsuranceQuoteHQ.com and fill out the simple form so that we can get you the quotes you need.
2. **Compare the insurance quotes carefully** and make sure that the quotes have the same coverage.

3. **<u>Buy the coverage</u>** you need at the most competitive rates.

4. Once you've completed the simple quote form and submitted it, come back to this website. Click on the SPECIAL REPORT nav button on the left of the page. When you leave your email address, I will instantly send you TWO SPECIAL REPORTS on buying Car Insurance:

- "5 Things To Do When Buying Car Insurance" (a $9.95 value)
- "5 Things To Avoid When Buying Car Insurance" (a $9.95 value)

**You will not spend one single cent!** They are my gift to you. The reports are available to anyone visiting this website with no cost or obligation.

**No other insurance quote site in the world** can offer you this winning formula for getting the best insurance rates AND maximizing your insurance claim settlements! No matter if your claim is a homeowners, renters, auto, business, etc...**THESE STRATEGIES WORK EVERY TIME!**

# Go NOW to: www.InsuranceQuoteHQ.com

RESERVED FOR ADVERTISER

www.ingramcontent.com/pod-product-compliance
Lightning Source LLC
Chambersburg PA
CBHW061152220326
41599CB00025B/4462